SIDELINE
CEO

Also by Marty Smith

Never Settle: Sports, Family, and the American Soul
(a *New York Times* bestseller)

SIDELINE
CEO

Leadership Principles
from Championship Coaches

MARTY SMITH

TWELVE

NEW YORK   BOSTON

Twelve
Hachette Book Group
1290 Avenue of the Americas, New York, NY 10104
twelvebooks.com
twitter.com/twelvebooks

First Edition: September 2023

Twelve is an imprint of Grand Central Publishing. The Twelve name and logo are trademarks of Hachette Book Group, Inc.

The publisher is not responsible for websites (or their content) that are not owned by the publisher.

The Hachette Speakers Bureau provides a wide range of authors for speaking events. To find out more, go to hachettespeakersbureau.com or email HachetteSpeakers@hbgusa.com.

Twelve books may be purchased in bulk for business, educational, or promotional use. For information, please contact your local bookseller or the Hachette Book Group Special Markets Department at special.markets@hbgusa.com.

Print book interior design by Bart Dawson

Library of Congress Control Number: 2023908381

ISBNs: 978-1-5387-5838-0 (hardcover), 978-1-5387-5840-3 (ebook)

Printed in the United States of America

LSC-C

Printing 1, 2023

To the leaders who pushed me beyond
what I believed was possible, thank you.
I wouldn't have this life without your belief in me.

CONTENTS

FOREWORD

It seems like every year there's another new book on what it means to be a successful leader!

As some will say, leadership is just another word for "influence." And I believe this to be true: Leadership is simply the ability to influence people.

Don't get me wrong, I believe the topic of leadership is important, but too many people (from what I've read) put it in a box. It looks like this or that. But as Marty shares in *Sideline CEO,* there are many forms of successful leadership and influence. It can take a variety of shapes and sizes. When Marty first shared the idea of his book with me, I was so intrigued. I thought, *Who wouldn't want to pick up a book about how some of the best leaders of all time do great things in different ways?* It's not a one-size-fits-all approach. Leaders can be big, small, short or tall, introverted or extroverted, a visionary, an operator—you name it!

In fact, if you want to talk about the most effective "leadership," it's probably manipulation. Yes, you read that correctly. One of the easiest and quickest ways to "lead" people is to lie and deceive. It's not right, but it's reality. It happens all the time. That's why I don't like talking about general leadership. I'm more interested in talking about leadership *that lasts.* And in *Sideline CEO,* Marty shares some of those things that lead to long-term impact.

Throughout my life, I've had the privilege of being on some great teams, and I've been employed by some great companies and mentored by some great people and coaches. One *Sideline* man I'll never forget is my high-school football coach, Coach Howard. He took a team that was everybody's "Homecoming game" and eventually led us to a state championship. Coach Howard had three team rules: Do what's right. Do your best. Treat everybody the way you want to be treated.

He would say, "It's my job to love you, and it's your job to love one another." I'm forever grateful for Coach Howard because he focused on building our character, not just developing us as athletes. He was a man who had *leadership that lasts.*

From what I've observed, if you want to impact people over time and have influence that spans generations, it starts with one thing: respect.

Notice I didn't say "like."

We live in a culture that cares so much about "likes" (social media, for instance). And unfortunately, we have conditioned ourselves to believe that our value and worth are determined by our post's popularity. "Likes" are fickle and fleeting, but *respect* is earned and can stand the test of time.

Our English word *respect* comes from a fourteenth-century Latin word meaning "to look back at." And as I look back at Marty Smith's career, I have the utmost respect for him. He is someone who speaks with conviction, works with great discipline, and has a deep sense of care for what he does. Working with him at ESPN over the years, I've seen Marty stand out among his peers because he never goes through the motions. He leads by example. You may not always "like" what he has to say about your favorite college football team or "like" his outfits on TV, but Marty is a man who earns the respect of people...even in his skinny jeans.

So if you're someone looking to learn from the best of the best, Marty's done the hard work for you. The following pages are the result of someone who has walked up and down the *sideline* listening to the things that make people great. Take advantage of his wisdom—and that of many others—and I believe you'll learn the qualities that make great leaders *last*.

"Leave the sides..."
Tim Tebow

SIDELINE
CEO

Chapter 1

LEADERSHIP

*"If you want to make everyone happy,
don't be a leader. Sell ice cream."*
—Steve Jobs, co-founder, Apple

Leadership. It is essential to conceptualizing, developing, growing, and sustaining any business. Confident direction from the top is essential, undeniable, hard to quantify and, sometimes, the greatest intangible.

Leadership can be lonely. And it's never easy.

It's not always William Wallace in *Braveheart* yelling "FREEDOM!" at the top of his lungs to motivate a legion. Sometimes it's a closed door and an open ear for a troubled soul, or the vulnerability and self-confidence to delegate responsibility in key moments to empower others. Sometimes it's an ass-chewing. Sometimes it's letting someone else run point in an important meeting. Sometimes it's presence during a silent ride home from practice.

Without strong leadership, failure is virtually inevitable. Rare is the unit that overcomes poor direction. Leadership includes myriad attributes and must possess a very fluid dynamic—what works with one group today may not motivate a different group tomorrow. Hell, what worked today may not motivate the *same* group tomorrow. What makes one person tick may turn someone else off. That's why tenured coaching leaders like Bill Belichick, Gregg Popovich, Dawn Staley, or Nick Saban are so fascinating. Think about who Saban was when he first became a head coach in 1990 at Toledo versus who he is today at Alabama. The evolution of the world, of society, of technology, of psychology, of relatability, of parenting styles, of operating rules, of the young people themselves, have all vastly changed during those decades.

So leadership has to adapt. Not leadership principles, necessarily, more so the execution thereof.

Every individual requires unique direction to find the best version of themselves. As a result, there is a certain clairvoyance required of individuals in leadership positions, because no two individuals are motivated in the exact same manner. You may have fifty employees. No two of them respond to the same stimulus exactly the same way.

We all have an innate understanding of what leadership does. *But what is it, exactly?* What are the attributes, qualities, personality traits, and experiences that develop great leaders? How is leadership built? And how is it cultivated and maintained?

How does it evolve over time, and how must you evolve with it to ensure its relevance and effectiveness? What are its supporting tentpoles and tactics? What percentage is muted psychology and what percentage is spittin'-mad motivation?

With age and experience, I began to wonder about these things. And I knew I had some resources to help uncover and extrapolate answers. My broadcasting position at ESPN affords me the tremendous opportunity to engage with some of the most successful, most prominent leaders in America and beyond—professional athletic coaches and executives—on a daily basis. These men and women shape and mold tomorrow's leaders on a globally visible, high-pressure scale, with annual roster turnover and astronomical expectations.

Sports is a performance-based business. In most instances, you either win or you're gone.

So if anyone knows how to define leadership and its key values, complete with unique, specific examples of its impact, it's them.

For this book, I spent hours interviewing coaching titans over a three-year span. I interviewed Doc Rivers as he rode the Philadelphia 76ers team bus to the arena. I interviewed Dabo Swinney during the forty-five-minute lull between events at one of my son's high school track meets. I interviewed Kim Mulkey minutes before she flew with her LSU Women's Basketball program to the 2023 NCAA Women's Final Four in Dallas, Texas. (Days later, Mulkey's Lady Tigers won the school's first women's basketball national championship.) These men and women scrapped and clawed and fought to earn and sustain pinnacle coaching positions. And as their careers blossomed, every person within these pages created an influential legacy of leadership excellence, both between the lines and beyond the game.

The idea for this project arose during the restless uncertainty of the COVID-19 pandemic. I don't sit still very well. Never have. Personally and professionally, all I have ever known is to grind. I was never the best athlete on my teams. I had to absorb my coaches' tutelage and work my ass off to maximize my ability. I am not the most talented television host or reporter. But I've never been outworked: This airplane to that assignment—next assignment, next airplane.

Home for a day or two, kiss Lainie and our kids, and gone again.

But during COVID, we all had no choice but to be still.

For the first time in my adult life, I was at home for months. And while Lainie and I were intentional about maximizing the blessing of undistracted time together and with our children, I, like many of you, was concerned about our future. I felt confused, anxious, and restless.

So I controlled what I could control. I went to work.

I'd had the book title in my head for a couple of years: *Sideline CEO*. It has a hell of a ring to it. And if *I* was at home with nothing but time, and desperately yearning for fellowship, I figured many of my coaching relationships felt the same. So, I picked up the phone and called University of North Carolina head football coach Mack Brown in Chapel Hill, North Carolina. Fifty-three minutes and change later, I'd attended a Master Class. The insight, vulnerability, candor, and experiential storytelling he shared with me suggested to me that this project had merit and just might resonate. Next, I called Urban Meyer, the former head football coach at The Ohio State University. His perspective left no doubt.

In total, twenty leaders shared their time and tutelage with me—many when they barely had time to offer, but they did so for the benefit of this book. For my benefit. I hope their brilliance resonates with you, and offers you perspective and consideration that you can apply to your own daily walk, just as I have.

Welcome to *Sideline CEO: Leadership Principles from Championship Coaches.*

ROY WILLIAMS (2007 Naismith Memorial Basketball Hall of Fame inductee; three-time National Champion Head Basketball Coach at the University of North Carolina): The definition of leadership is a question I ask myself all the time, because it constantly evolves. The biggest and easiest way to define leadership is to look at people's words and actions, and see how many people follow them. See how many people trust them. I tend to complicate it, but leadership is simple, really—it's the guy everyone else will follow anywhere, anytime, because that person earned their loyalty by trust of his words or trust of his actions.

JOHN CALIPARI (2015 Naismith Memorial Basketball Hall of Fame inductee; National Champion Head Basketball Coach at the University of Kentucky): Leadership is helping people get to where they're capable of going—even when they're not sure they can get there themselves.

TOM IZZO (2016 Naismith Memorial Basketball Hall of Fame inductee; National Champion Head Basketball Coach at Michigan State University): Leadership for me is getting guys to do things they don't believe they're capable of doing. And that's a simple statement but a complicated challenge.

NICK SABAN (Seven-time National Champion Head Football Coach at the University of Alabama and Louisiana State

University): I think the only thing I've had to do as a leader is make it about the players [I'm leading]. So, define goals and aspirations for what they want to accomplish and what they want to achieve. And then I want them to understand—and clearly define—what do they have to do to accomplish that? And how do they have to edit their behavior to be able to do it? And can they have the discipline to execute it every day? I'm talking about self-discipline, now. We make hundreds of decisions every day that come down to two questions. Number one: "There's something I know I'm supposed to do, but I really don't want to do." Do you do it? And number two: "There's something over here that I know I'm *not* supposed to do, but I want to do it." Do you do it?

LANE KIFFIN (Ole Miss Head Football Coach; National Champion offensive coordinator at the University of Alabama): *(laughing)* That's Nick Saban 101, right there. Coach Saban always used to say that statement to the entire team every Friday going into the weekend, about discipline and decision-making. And listen, he could say it, and everybody listens because that guy lives it. He was an undeniable example for leadership about how to be disciplined. I tell everybody: Coaches say stuff all the time to their players, but Coach Saban *lives* it. He exudes discipline in every area of life. His leadership approach and dedication had a major impact on me.

NICK SABAN: Those kinds of personal self-disciplines are really the most difficult thing to sustain. But if you can do that, you're always going to make the right choices and stay on path to accomplish the goals that you have. So, as the leader I try to work on mindset, and the mindset is really about the individual becoming the best that they can be.

DOC RIVERS (2008 NBA Champion Head Coach of the Boston Celtics; former head coach of the Philadelphia 76ers): I would say leadership is consistent. Leadership is not a democracy. Teams aren't a democracy. But there are attributes of leadership that have to be consistent. You don't treat everybody the exact same. Leadership, at times, can be very lonely and it can be very unpopular. But if it's coming from the right place, from a place with no personal agenda, then leadership is powerful. People follow when they know their leader doesn't have an agenda, except for what the *team* agenda is.

DABO SWINNEY (Two-time National Champion Head Football Coach, Clemson University): Leadership comes down to this: If your actions and your habits motivate and inspire others to want to do more, be more, dream more, then you're a leader.

GREG SANKEY (1991 Golf Coaches Association of America Region VI Co-Coach of the Year, Northwestern State University; *see also:* The Southeastern Conference

Commissioner): Leadership is influence. And that doesn't mean power.

KIM MULKEY (2020 Naismith Memorial Basketball Hall of Fame inductee; four-time National Champion Women's Basketball Coach at Louisiana State University and Baylor University; currently at LSU): There's several definitions of leadership. And there's several ways you can lead. But first, you have to figure out your own personality and not try to be someone you're not. A leader has to stand before people in such a way that those people want to follow. What will make someone follow you? If they see that you're leading them in the right direction, that you believe in what you're doing, you *know* what you're doing. And you get results.

NANCY LIEBERMAN (1996 Naismith Memorial Basketball Hall of Fame inductee): Leadership is constantly and consistently giving somebody a reason to follow you. Not because you make more money than them. Not because you have a better title. But because you're deep, you're obsessed with excellence, you're wise, you have intensity, you're determined and passionate, you listen, and you're willing to take care of the people you lead.

FRANK BEAMER (2018 College Football Hall of Fame inductee; Big East Conference and Atlantic Coast Conference Champion Head Football Coach at Virginia Tech): A leader is someone of high integrity, who has great communication skills and is highly organized. A leader has to be who they really are, has to be genuine. And for me, this is critically important in leadership: A leader never embarrasses a player in front of his peers or coaches. That was always an important part of my leadership approach.

URBAN MEYER (Three-time National Champion Head Football Coach at the University of Florida and at The Ohio State University): As a leader, you can't just say you're going to fix a problem. You have to lead when there's a problem or you're going to fail. So that means you have to confront the problem or failure and demand the problem is addressed and rectified, and then follow through to confirm it is addressed and rectified. If you don't do that, you're not a leader.

TOM IZZO: I've spent time with Urban Meyer. His confront-and-demand concept is unbelievable, because I think real leaders confront people. There's not many people who have the guts to confront people. But Urban takes it a step further: Leaders confront, but real leaders demand that what you've confronted gets carried through. That is critical.

MACK BROWN (2018 College Football Hall of Fame inductee; two-time National Champion Head Football Coach at the University of Texas, now at the University of North Carolina): Leadership to me is two- or threefold, but number one, it's taking crises and turning them into positives. Because as a CEO, as a head football coach, you deal with so many different people, and your job has so much diversity that you're going to have crises. It's inevitable. And instead of running and hiding from them, or panicking every time one comes up, what you've got to do is figure it out. That's your job.

TOM IZZO: We get some guys who confront issues that need to be addressed. But then I say, "Did you follow up? Did you demand that he did what you confronted him about?" That's so important. That way it's not an idle threat. I think, in general, we've become such a weak and soft society that we don't confront and demand because there's not as many good leaders.

URBAN MEYER: The definition I used for leadership for many years was to set a standard and demand all live up to that standard. I call that the 1970s version. That's very shallow. You don't demand anything nowadays. So, the new and improved version is, a leader has to earn trust, and then with great clarity equip and inspire others to live up to those standards. The key points are this: Earn trust, equip, and inspire. That's what a leader today has to do. The best leaders earn trust, and they equip and inspire those that they're trying to lead. Notice: There's no more "demand" in there. That's not the way the world works anymore.

TIM CORBIN (Two-time National Champion Head Baseball Coach at Vanderbilt University): When it gets down to it, leadership is the ability to learn how to serve, and to draw people in, emotionally, toward a group effort. We don't have captains on my teams. If I ever did have captains on a team, it would be voted on at the end of the year, after the experience was over. Because I've always felt like real leadership happens through the experience, through the environment. True leadership is the ability to model the standards and behaviors of an organization. It's more about looking out for other people than anything else.

CHRISTIAN HORNER (Eleven-time Formula 1 World Champion Team Principal—six driver, five constructor; currently CEO, Team Principal, Red Bull F1): In leadership, you set the tempo and the example. And *the* key attribute is being able to communicate openly, honestly, effectively, to build an effective group of people around you.

JIMBO FISHER (National Champion Head Football Coach at Florida State University, currently head football coach at Texas A&M University): Leadership is giving direction and confidence and instruction with great value in your words, that results in giving people confidence to be able to know that they can do their job. And that includes times when they don't believe they have the ability to do it themselves.

MACK BROWN: First you try to keep crises from happening, get ahead of it. But if it costs you, and you're in trouble with it, you stop it, you're honest, you fix it, and you move forward and learn from it and make it as positive as you can. The other variables great leaders possess are being self-confident and having a confident plan, making people believe in you, making people want to follow you. And in my estimation, a good leader makes everyone around you do what you think is the best thing to do, while making them feel like it's their idea. It's got to be all-inclusive.

TOM IZZO: Real leaders are trying to push people, trying to pull people, constantly encouraging people to do things beyond what anyone ever thought they could do. Including themselves. A lot of people dream about what they can do, but naturally don't—or won't—do it. And to me, a leader is one that brings other people with you.

PATTY GASSO (Seven-time National Champion Head Softball Coach at the University of Oklahoma; 2012 National Fastpitch Coaches Association Hall of Fame inductee): I've learned through my time as a coach that leadership is about relationships. And there is a fine line, in the way of understanding that I'll meet you halfway, but I'm not trying to be your best friend. I want players to feel like, "If I need something I'm going to call her, because I know I'm safe with her; I'm not afraid to tell her what I need to tell her because she's not going to reprimand me." But there's a measure of respect required. I want you to feel comfortable with telling me what you need to say. I want them to know that I'm here to make them, first, the best human they can be through lessons learned, but also help push them to be the best athlete they can be. And sometimes that means pushing them past what they think they can be.

GREG SANKEY: There are probably fifty definitions for leadership. I tell people what I want to be is influential and effective. So, whether you're trying to get a friend to go with you someplace or lead a group of people in an organization to accomplish a goal in order to achieve an objective, you're trying to influence them in a certain direction. And then the question is: Are you effective at that? To me, that's the essence of leadership.

DABO SWINNEY: You can be smart, intelligent, and you can lead an organization. But that doesn't necessarily make you a great *leader*. There's a difference. There's a difference in leading and being a great *leader*. A leader is someone who people truly want to follow. Other people may not necessarily be great leaders, but they're in a position of leadership. They may be able to lead strategically or lead from a business acumen, decision-making standpoint. But that doesn't make them a leader. To me, a leader has a high level of trust and respect, and uncompromising integrity that people are drawn to and want to follow. Those are the best leaders.

JOE GIBBS (1996 Pro Football Hall of Fame inductee; three-time NFL Super Bowl Champion Head Coach; 2020 NASCAR Hall of Fame inductee; five-time NASCAR Cup Series Champion car owner): The leader sets the standard for what you're trying to accomplish. And to me, the most effective leaders are servant-style leaders. In other words, the best way to lead is you're there early, you stay late, and you're constantly getting after it yourself. It's awful easy to just give direction to other people. But it's better to show them through action that you're in it with them.

JOHN CALIPARI: Leadership is taking the players you're leading with you. And part of that leadership is, the players are *always* watching. So it's your actions as much as what you say. Maybe more. How you deal with things. How you approach things daily. Consistency. But I would say, for me, it's getting people to go to places they're capable of going, but they're not sure they can get there.

TOM IZZO: I tell you what I hate. I hate when people say, "He leads by example." I hate when I have a parent that always says to me, "Hey, my son's a leader." And I say, "What do you mean he's a leader?" He says, "He's a 3.8 [grade point average] student. He works out every day. He does this. He does that. He's a hell of a leader." And I say, "Your son is not a leader. He's in the gym by himself. He studies by himself." A leader *must* influence other people. So I hate the term "He leads by example." That only means nobody else is watching. And if nobody else is watching he ain't leading nobody. He's just leading himself. So I'd say a real definition, a leader is somebody who brings other people with them.

JIMBO FISHER: Leading is about the effect you have on the other people. Some guys are real vocal, but just okay leaders. Other guys can be quiet. It gets down to how you affect the guys on your team positively every day, and at what consistency level. You have to, in leadership, get across what you're trying to instill in them, the information you're trying to relay or what you want them to do. And you've gotta live it. *Live. It.*

TIM CORBIN: Leadership...I don't think everyone is cut out for it. I do think everyone has the ability to learn it. I think everyone has the ability to try to understand it. And if it's something that raises your emotions, then I think you'll have the ability to follow through on it. But leadership is fluid. There's a lot of responsibility to it. It requires a lot of emotional and mental energy. And it's not something you do just when the feeling or the mood is right. It has to be on the front of your brain. If leadership is something that's very important to you, then you understand the communication that exists in your life, whether it's verbal, it's listening, or it's modeling, it all applies. It's habit. There's an awareness level of a leader that has to be different, because you have to be very, very aware of your own being and you certainly have to be very aware of the people around you, and the environment you're in.

LEONARD HAMILTON (Big East Conference and Atlantic Coach Conference Champion men's basketball coach; currently at Florida State University): It's academic to have nine leadership points of this, or nine leadership points of that, but leadership is not always putting it down on paper. It's your forward thinking. It's your sensitivity to everyone else's needs. It's your ability to adapt and be patient when things are not going well. And it's trying to teach when everyone has a different learning skill. What I might expose you to, and expose him to, you might pick up, and he might be just as smart as you but he doesn't learn the same way. So as the leader, I've got to find a method that works for him. And as the leader, I've got to be sensitive to those differences.

TOM IZZO: It used to be, when I started, your title gave you seniority. It gave you power. Now, the president of the United States, coaches, everybody...We [as a society] rip everybody! Your title doesn't matter! Parents get ripped. Your title does not get you a hall pass. You have to earn trust with every group that comes in. If you're a five-star general, everybody just respected you. Not anymore.

ROY WILLIAMS: Nobody cares what you did. They care what you do.

NANCY LIEBERMAN: Leaders have to answer the *why*. Why are we doing this? Your ego is not your amigo. And you can have confidence and high levels of self-esteem, but you also have to humble yourself to develop genuine relationships with the people you lead.

URBAN MEYER: Leadership now is relationship-based. Back when I started coaching it was authority-based. I grew up with Woody Hayes, Earl Bruce, my father. It was authoritarian. It was simple: You do this *because I'm telling you to do this.* That's the way my career started. When I was a high school player, yes, you had a relationship with the coach. But that relationship was, he's the coach, you're the player, and you do what they say to do. That's it. Period. That was the extent of the relationship. Same way with parents. Be home at ten o'clock or you're gonna get your ass beat in! The teacher told you to shut up or she was going to kick your ass out of class. It was authoritarian. Now it's very relationship-based.

MACK BROWN: You'd better make time for the people you're leading. It has to be personal.

ROY WILLIAMS: Leadership is twenty-four-hour devotion to our team in everything I do. For me, it's my family and basketball. That's it. Nothing else. And my devotion is toward this basketball team. And I'm going to make every decision based on what is best for that basketball team, with one addendum, and it's a very important addendum: I also realize that all of the players have their own individual dreams and goals, too. That's very important.

TOM IZZO: If someone asked me what I think I do best here at Michigan State, it's not recruit, it's not coach my guys—it's that I *spend time* with my guys. I spend time learning who they are as young men. Times changed. I grew up in Iron Mountain [Michigan], man, a tough, blue-collar environment. That's all we knew. The Vince Lombardi era. And the Vince Lombardi era was, I'm going to line you up, and I'm going to tell you to run through a brick wall. And you're going to run through that brick wall and you're going to ask questions later. So when I got this job I thought, *How can I keep the Vince Lombardi theory with the new way of doing things?* So I said, "I'm going to line you up, I'm going to tell you *why* you should run through that brick wall. Because the objective is to get through the brick wall. The objective is not *how* you get through the brick wall." You have to get to the other side of the wall. I always thought the only way you can do that is, you've got to get guys to trust you. And trust requires time.

JOHN CALIPARI: A good leader can move things for different reasons. The great ones lead people enthusiastically in the right direction, while knowing they're being led. I call it "servant leadership," where the player knows without question, "This is about me." That's when they become enthusiastic people within the organization, when they believe—when they *know*—it's about them. In my mind, those are the guys and ladies who are great leaders, when you can move people.

JIMBO FISHER: Leadership varies. Because you have to learn to understand how certain people interpret things. I'm not going to treat everybody the same. I'm gonna treat every-body fairly. Because people are different. They're different per-sonalities, and they interpret things differently. And I think you have to coach each player differently as a result. Each individual has a certain organizational standard they have to live up to. You can't deviate from that standard. Because for success, reaching that standard is what we have to do. But each individual, getting him to see what he's got to see—and how he's got to see it—to meet that standard, will be different with each individual guy. So you, as the leader, have to figure out the best way to reach them.

JOHN CALIPARI: Sometimes you move your players by being mean and nasty. But when you move them when it's about them, when you move them based on the belief you have in them—and they know it—they know you're invested in their well-being. [Former Kentucky forward] Nick Richards came in for the last meeting we had with him, and that was his comment—"You guys believed in me when I didn't believe in myself, and you stuck with me. And I love you for it." That's what we try to do. That's the essence of how we try to lead.

URBAN MEYER: The greatest leaders, especially in this gen-eration, are those that genuinely care for those they're lead-ing. Not just say they care, but genuinely care. Not driven by narratives, not driven by media or how it's going to look to the outside world. And I've seen coaches that are driven by those other things. Great coaches have one concern—their team. That single-minded focus. The leaders who have that sole focus are the ones that win.

MACK BROWN: I went to Iraq in 2008, and I spent ten days there. There were a lot of generals over there. I spent an hour and a half with General Raymond Odierno. I asked him, "Do you recruit leaders or do you make leaders?" He said, "You make leaders. Why do you think we have academies?" He said, "I'm really concerned right now that we're spending so much time in war, that we're spending more time fighting than we are teaching. And I'm really concerned about our leadership going forward." He told me, "You'll have a lot of leaders on your team. Your best leader may be a bad leader, but kids follow him. So you've got to be really careful that your best leader is not a guy that's hurting you more than anything else." He told me I should constantly teach leadership. The way to do that is to bring in people that you admire, that you emulate, and have them constantly talking to your team, doing seminars with your team. That applies to every team. We start practice with a team meeting every single day. Every day. Without fail. We never have a practice without a team meeting. And I start every practice off with a thought of the day. And then I follow the thought up with a conversation about how that thought relates to us today. And then I'm constantly talking to them about me as a leader, their coaches as leaders, them as leaders. It is a constant narrative. To be an effective leader, it has to be.

LEONARD HAMILTON: You could call it leadership. Or you could say wisdom. Who we are is the result of the experiences we've had in our lives. So for me, being the oldest child from my mother's second marriage, I had three brothers and a sister under me. My leadership started early. Because I realized that my siblings would probably develop in relationship to how they saw me developing. So I had added responsibility that was in part of my being. At twelve years old I'm babysitting my brothers and sister while my parents were working. When you ask me about leadership, you're asking me from where I am now. But people who are good leaders, those skills start developing at a much younger age, when they don't even know that the circumstances they're living in allows them to have that leadership possibility. So now, as you get older and more mature, those mindsets they had to deal with as youngsters have a big part in how they respond to things. And being in that situation with my brothers and sister, the circumstances we operated in—eight of us living in a two-bedroom house, four guys on two bunkbeds, the bathroom on the back porch, taking my bath in a tin tub in the corner, no hot or cold running water—I'm operating from survival. We're just trying to survive! How am I going to get me, and us, out of this situation, where we don't have to live like this anymore? When you live in that environment, it's survival of the fittest. You're always aware. So in order for you to understand me and my leadership skills, and how they developed, you have to understand that environment. You have to understand where I come from.

ROY WILLIAMS: Tyler Hansbrough [former North Carolina forward; 2008 Naismith National Player of the Year] is a great example of powerful leadership from within the program. He was a four-time First Team All-American. If he said, "Come on guys!," that was about all it took. His teammates followed him. They listened to him. The respect was obvious because it was earned. Because every frickin' drill we ever did—every stinkin' one of them for four years—he tried to kill people. He tried to win every sprint. And he didn't ease up when he knew he was going to make the required time. No. It was all-out, all the time. He just tried to kill everybody in everything that we did. So what's that do? How does that prove leadership? People followed that. People said, "Okay, that guy is the leader. And that's what he does? That's his personal standard? Then that's what we've got to do." It's hard for a guy to talk the talk and then not do it on the court. If a guy says, "Come on guys, you need to do this or that," but doesn't do it himself in the arena, he has no following. None.

LANE KIFFIN: Let me tell you when I realized I had to practice what I preach. I made a decision to change my life after the [2021] Outback Bowl, when I saw a picture of the players throwing the Gatorade on me. I looked so fat. I looked like an anaconda snake when it swallows an animal, and the animal gets stuck in their neck. So, I'm like, I'm doing something to fix this. So, my doctor explains to me that there's a cleanse in which there is no alcohol, no red meat, and no bread. I started it for ten or fourteen days, and the competitiveness in me said,

All right, this feels amazing, let's keep going. That led up to the next season, and I was still doing the cleanse. Matt Corral [former Ole Miss All-SEC quarterback] was asking me about it. And Matt said he thought the cleanse would be really cool to do and asked if I would match him if he did the cleanse all season. I said sure, it's easy for me. I'm already eight or nine months into it. But here's the interesting thing: I learned so much from Matt during that time. It was amazing to watch a college student, not just in Oxford, Mississippi, but anywhere, do that with all the peer pressure, the weekends partying, and all those normal things. And I just saw the clarity in him emerge, because of that decision to drink no alcohol. It was the ultimate clarity of a season, coach and quarterback working in unison to do something together. It was really neat to see. Players respect decisions like that a lot, because they know how unusual it is to make a decision like that. And there's another layer here, too, when you talk about leadership and setting examples for the people you're leading. I remember saying, "Hey, linemen, you gotta get in shape if you're gonna play in our fast tempo offense." At our end-of-the-year meeting with two of our linemen who were overweight, I'm telling them, "Look, you guys gotta have discipline, man. You can't eat like you are. You gotta change your diet and what you're putting in your body." And I'm sitting there at the same time thinking, *What am I doing? I'm saying this to them, but here I am doing it myself.* That was part of it, too. I just thought it was hypocritical to go up in front of these guys and preach discipline and decision-making, and having the discipline to not do the things you want to do that you know you shouldn't do, and doing things you don't want to do but you should do, and following through and doing them. How hypocritical can you be? Did you hear that? Nick Saban 101. I sound just like him. You think he had an influence on me as a leader?

KIM MULKEY: When you lead people, you have to interact with the entire team, but also have to know a little bit about everyone that's a part of that team. Because what motivates you doesn't motivate the guy next to you. When I look at leaders, I don't necessarily look at how they lead. I look at production. What have they done in their life? What are the results? To me, those are the types of leaders I want to follow. I may not always agree with things leaders do, but if the results are positive and powerful, sometimes you just need to follow.

JIMBO FISHER: It's hard to follow a leader you don't trust. Trust is the ultimate factor in leadership. They have to trust that you have their best interests at heart no matter how hard you coach them, how easy you coach them, and in everything you tell them.

GREG SANKEY: As a leader you have to make decisions about communication, timing, information, subject matter, all in an effort to figure out how to have influence and be effective. That can be a very lonely position sometimes.

URBAN MEYER: It's amazing to me. Some of the mistakes—and I'm not throwing any daggers at all, because trust me, I've made them all—but when I go visit places and I'll talk to the coach and a lot of the athletes, and when you're too rigid and you don't adapt to the kind of team you have, that's going to be a very poor ending.

ROY WILLIAMS: I tell my players, if you're willing to work as hard as I'm going to work, we're going to have something very special and we're going to be successful. But I've never had a player yet to work as hard as I'm going to work. Don't just tell them. Show them. It is twenty-four-hour devotion to our team in everything I do.

MACK BROWN: Leaders can't have bad days. You can't say, "I don't feel good." You can't say, "Man, I'm off my game today." That mess doesn't exist. And you've got to be the hardest worker. They have to see you want it. I'm the first one in our building and the last one to leave, and every last one of them knows that and sees that. I recruit harder than any of them, and every one of them knows that. I'm constantly talking to our staff about what leadership means, too. That never turns off. You have to coach your coaches. I tell my coaches, you can't go out and get drunk with your buddies and then tell your players not to drink.

JOHN CALIPARI: When you're the head of an organization, you feel a sense of responsibility to everyone below. From every assistant to every secretary to every trainer, everyone, you feel a sense of responsibility to do your best for them to lead the organization in a way that they will all benefit. To be that person that they know, and they're excited that this is the organization they work in. When you're at a job like Kentucky, it's much bigger than just coaching basketball. If you're here, and you're in the seat that I'm in, and you don't use it to do good away from the court, and away from what you do, you're cheating the position. Some of us have been put in positions undeservedly. I don't know why I got the Kentucky job. I wasn't that kind of a player. I didn't play for this guy, and didn't coach under that guy, and I got the Kentucky job. But what I do know is I'm in a position to make a difference with other people, in different causes and different things. And I think you want everybody in the organization to see all of that. You do have a sense of responsibility for a lot more than just yourself—and you feel that responsibility every single day.

JIMBO FISHER: There are many kinds of leadership. But at the end of the day, people want to know:

- You know what you're talking about, and . . .
- You know how to articulate what you know and get it across, so they can learn it and apply it, and how it can help them get better. And that they believe that I have complete and utter trust in what I say. That's the thing leadership gets down to, trust.

Smith's Sideline Summary: Leadership

- Leadership is directing people to achieve their optimum potential, even when those people may not believe they're capable.
- Leadership is influence, not power.
- Leadership is consistent.
- Leaders cannot have bad days, and leaders do not get days off.
- Leadership is not for everyone. If you're concerned with popularity, or making everyone happy, leadership is not for you. If you are insecure or indecisive about your direction or conviction, or unwilling to confront failure, poor attitudes, or lack of discipline, leadership is not for you. Some individuals are born to lead and taught how to lead. Some don't want the responsibility. Some can't handle the responsibility.
- Good leaders have an intrinsic work ethic, unyielding determination, and fearlessness to confront others who do not share the same conviction.
- If leaders fail, they work. If leaders succeed, they work harder.
- Leaders expect excellence, not perfection. Approaches to that end often vary. Principles rarely do.
- Servant leadership is effective leadership: Show me, don't tell me.

Chapter 2

TRUST

"Trust is the highest form of human motivation. It brings out the very best in people."
—Stephen R. Covey, author, *The 7 Habits of Highly Successful People*

Without trust, no relationship is authentic. Without trust, there can be no emotional depth. Emotional depth is a requisite for complete buy-in.

Many leaders will tell you trust is the most important variable in leadership. It requires honesty, vulnerability, and consistency. Individuals you lead must genuinely believe—*they must know!*—that what you say is true and that you will follow through on those words.

If we don't trust, we don't believe.

If we don't believe, we're not truly invested.

And if we're not truly invested, we cannot win.

Trust is *the* most vital foundation principle required to galvanize groups of individuals toward a common goal and is the pathway to lasting personal relationships.

Trust is hard to earn.

Trust is easy to lose.

Trust development and maintenance is like wattage output during an intense cardiovascular workout. Take Peloton, for example. When I'm on that bike and I turn that red knob to the right to increase the required effort, I watch the average wattage output climb slowly and methodically. Then, if I continue to focus on producing a solid effort, I maintain a consistent wattage average. The effort sustains the output. But the moment I turn that red knob to the left, choose an easier path, slack off on the effort even slightly or—heaven forbid—take a break altogether, the wattage output plummets.

Everything I worked so hard to build suffers when I stop giving intentional consistent effort, focus, and intensity.

Same with trust.

It is difficult to build. It takes time and effort and resolve and patience and consistency. But it will wane quickly if we compromise the effort and stop trying as hard.

KIRBY SMART (Two-time National Champion Head Football Coach, University of Georgia): You cannot have leadership without trust. That's where leadership begins and ends.

ROY WILLIAMS: Trust is telling the truth and following through. And if you don't do that, you don't last very long.

DOC RIVERS: You don't earn leadership before you earn trust. When you have trust in leadership and in culture, you have an opportunity to reach people and to win.

MACK BROWN: Without building trust and respect—which is easy to say and hard to do—you're dead in the water. Without trust, you have no chance. You're done. That includes respect for yourself, respect for your opponent, respect for the game. Trust: Is there any question that when I tell you something, you're going to 100 percent believe that it's true? To achieve that level of trust, I've got to do it every single time I tell them that. I must do what I told them I was going to do. Every time. So if I tell [University of North Carolina athletics director] Bubba Cunningham I promised these kids something, and then don't do it? I'm quitting. Because I've lost who I am. I have to be 100 percent committed to the truth.

DOC RIVERS: *Trust* is an action word. Trust is built and shown through *action*. And everybody trusts differently. As a coach, you have to know that. Some people give you trust. Some people, trust has to be earned. And everybody's level of trusting, and way of trusting is different. It's always gonna be that way. And trust never stops. You can never stop earning trust and working for it. But it's also a two-way street. It can't be just one-way. You just can't give trust. You have to trust, as well.

KIM MULKEY: Trust comes with time—and you can't rush time. I'm not going to trust you until I observe and watch you in action for a while. Trust is a problem I have in my own personal life. I don't trust a lot of people. My circle is very small. I have to be around you. I have to watch you in action.

KIRBY SMART: If the people you're leading don't trust and believe everything you say to them, you can't lead them. Trust is earned. It's not given. I don't think you can put a value on trust in leadership. One of the most important things I've learned as a leader is that time spent away from football is time in the trust bank. The trust bank gives me confidence from the players I'm leading, so I've got to put the right amount of time in the bank with them, so that when the time comes and they have to trust me, they will trust me and follow the message. But you can't earn trust without the commitment of time.

NANCY LIEBERMAN: There's nothing more valuable than trust. Whether you're in a marriage or a relationship, business, sports, war, in the foxhole, or you're on a team, trust is the ultimate attribute. Trust says that you will be there for me no matter what happens, and that's an extraordinary thing. Trust is [being] consistent, and not being a "Dow Joneser" who is up and down. Trust means you're as loyal as a dog. Dogs are reliable. They have truth. They have strength. And you want the people you're leading to know you will be there always, not just when it's convenient. In fact, you want every person in your life to know that. Building that and sustaining that takes effort and follow-through.

GREG SANKEY: The value of trust in leadership is very high. Trust is very important, and it's also a two-way street. The word is one thing. Living it is another. There will be moments as a leader where there may be a level of trust that is broken, and you're going to have to invest to rebuild that. It's not just a linear concept. You're going to make mistakes as a leader. And you're probably going to have to withdraw from the trust bank. So you have to make consistent deposits in that trust bank to build and develop the deep level of trust that's necessary to truly lead people.

PATTY GASSO: Trust is very high at the top of the leadership value scale. If I can't trust a player, I feel like I can't put them in a lineup. They've got to be all in as a teammate, and we've worked very hard on understanding that. As a program, we're not flashing our rings or trophies. It's a humble, blue-collar style. And as a blue-collar-type worker, you have to trust who's around you, and they have to trust you in order to make it work. I need the players to trust me, as well. So I have to watch what I say. If I say one thing and do another, there's no trust. I have to always lead by example. Whether I'm having a good day or not, they're not going to know it. And that's something that I always push myself to make sure I'm paying attention to my mood and the things that I'm saying because I don't want to be high one day and low another. Inconsistency is where you lose trust. If I'm speaking out of both sides of my mouth, they're not going to trust me. But trust is extremely important as a team, to know that everybody on the field has worked their tails off to be there. And with games, we make mistakes. But through trust you get over those mistakes. If you put somebody on the field who you're uncomfortable with, and they're not properly focused, it's a detriment to the team. So I'm trying to get twenty athletes that are all in as often as I can. Without trust both ways, that can't happen.

JIMBO FISHER: People have to know you're all in with them. Players say it's a dictatorship. No, it's not! They say, "Well, Coach, you've got my future in your hands!" And I say, "Well, you've got *my* future in *your* hands!" We're in this thing together. But here's the other thing: I'm fifty-seven years old. I've been through things like this before. You haven't. My experience is where you've got to trust me. Why would I tell you something wrong, or that would be detrimental to you, or wasn't in your best interests, if it doesn't lead both of us toward the goal that we want? Building that trust, that I want what's best for you always, is how you win.

TIM CORBIN: Trust is the component needed for a relationship to move forward. My experience of being a stepparent really gave me a profound understanding of trust as it pertains to teaching and coaching. Maggie [Corbin's wife] and I dated for four years, and I knew I loved her. She knew she loved me. And we both knew we were going to marry one another. But the reason we didn't marry one another sooner was because we wanted to give the relationship time with the girls. And the girls were young at the time, but my main thought process was, if this is really going to work and we become a family, there needs to be time taken so that the girls trust me as an individual and someone who's going to be in their home. So we didn't rush that. I didn't try to replace anyone, just tried to blend into the family. When you learn to love someone else's children, it builds a philosophy of what

I'm doing right now. Because essentially you're taking on the responsibility of someone else's child.

But in the recruiting process you do not develop trust. You might start it, but you develop trust in your everyday interaction with the team and with individuals. That, too, takes a lot of time. Because if you are going to develop trust with one another, there is a lot of communication and listening that goes on between the parties. You can't tell them that they're *going to* trust you. You can't tell them *to* trust you. It's earned by daily interaction and daily progression. And then once trust starts to happen, real teaching can take place. It can start. But I don't think the other party really internalizes it until they understand where your compass is pointed. Is it pointed toward them? Is it pointed toward the team? Do they understand you enough to know who you really are and what you mean as a teacher? You can't force-feed them. You have to do it in time. Trust takes time. It takes a lot of interaction. It's not built overnight. It might be a couple of bricks in the house, but the house takes time to build to completion. Trust requires that daily progression. Over and over.

JOHN CALIPARI: Trust, in the profession I'm in, is built in the recruiting process. If you embellish, if you lie, if you paint a false picture that you know is not true; if you make promises you cannot keep; if you're promising everybody the same stuff; when they come to campus they talk, and then they immediately know you lied. And now you got no trust.

ROY WILLIAMS: Everybody who comes to play basketball at the University of North Carolina thinks they're going to be an NBA player, so I can never forget their own individual goals. If I get Team Goal and Individual Goal as Priority 1 and 1A, I've also developed trust with them because they know I'm going to appreciate their personal goals, too, and not throw those individual goals out the window and never be concerned about them. That's part of trust. And caring for someone else's aspirations applies to any relationship.

LANE KIFFIN: I'm certain I will be an outlier when it comes to my thoughts on the value of trust. If you're a great recruiter, you can get away with a lot of things. Sports are different than the normal world. Because in sports, the number one, absolute most important thing, is talent. You can overcome trust issues with talent. I've seen places where there's not a lot of trust and they still win a ton of games. The reason why is great players. Now, that said, always with players—and nowadays more than ever—the players don't automatically trust people. So I do think trust is a value. It's a value especially when things don't go well, and you're having a rough season or injuries or a couple of losses where the media is critical. And when the players don't trust you, that's when you get in trouble. So don't get me wrong: Trust is really important. I just personally believe that in many cases talent is more important. Talent can make you look like one hell of a leader.

TOM IZZO: That line you hear all the time: I want to play for a player-coach. To me, I can put myself down as a player-coach, because I spend time with my guys and I demand of them. I demand of them because I've got a license to—because I spend time with them. That's a mistake some people make. You can't go chew a kid's ass you have no relationship with. He's blowing you off. Or, even worse, he's leaving. But if you've shown him why you can help him and follow through, they'll take a bullet for you, man. That's trust, coach. *That* is trust.

JOHN CALIPARI: If they know you care and they have any doubt that you're not telling the truth, if they have any doubt that you told them this, that, and the other, and none of it came true, you're done. And I think a lot of trust, too, comes from spending individual time with kids, whether it be on the court individually, in the office individually, trying to feel out where they are and let them know, look, I care about you.

ROY WILLIAMS: Trust is gained by people realizing you care about them as a person and as an individual, and you will advise them about what's best for them as an individual. And that that advice may not help your goals [as coach] or your team—and may, in fact, hurt your goals or your team.

FRANK BEAMER: When you tell people information, they have to trust that you're telling them what you believe. Integrity and trust go hand in hand. I never told a player intentionally something I knew wasn't true. Because after you don't tell the truth the first time, then every time after that, when you're telling them something, that person can't trust that they can believe you. You can't lead them if they can't trust what you tell them.

JIMBO FISHER: Consistency and honesty build trust. We may agree to disagree, and you may not like what I have to say, but I'm always going to be consistent and I'm always going to be honest—and I'm always going to tell you what I think is best for your future. I'm not saying either one of us don't make mistakes. But at the end of the day it's consistency, honesty, and sincerity of what you tell somebody. And knowledge. If you have knowledge in what you're doing, you can articulate when you have those difficult conversations or situations with people. That builds trust.

JOHN CALIPARI: You may be able to intimidate them into playing, but they really don't trust you.

TOM IZZO: Trust is harder to get now. Some kids, we might be the first male figure in their life that's getting on their ass. They don't like that shit. They've never had their ass chewed. That's why we have to get kids to trust us. It's the most important part of leadership. A lot of coaches don't want to spend the time you need in order to build it. In basketball it's harder than it is in football. That's why you better empower some of your assistants and all be on the same page.

ROY WILLIAMS: Trust is the biggest thing in leadership. I've had so many players say, "Coach was always about our team, but never lost sight of each individual." That's something I've always appreciated to hear.

URBAN MEYER: I've worked with a leadership consultant named Tim Kight. Starting in 2012, we teach our coaches how to earn trust. We call it the Triad of Trust.

The first thing is **Character Trust**. Always remember: As leaders you are not measured by your intentions—you are measured by your actions. So with trust, this person has to have repeated experiences of you doing something. For example: Character Trust is repeated experiences of doing what you say you're going to do. So if you're coaching a team, that team has to feel that when you say something you're going to do it. And I've made many mistakes. I've heard, especially now that I travel around and coaches have me come in and I listen and learn, that coaches have a tendency to talk too much. For example: If you're an assistant coach, and you tell a kid he's going to play ten plays in the next game if he works real hard, and it just happens that he doesn't play those ten plays, then in that kid's mind you're a liar. And you just lost trust. So it's important to be very cautious with what you say. Character Trust is repeated experiences of doing what you say you're going to do.

The next part of trust is **Competency Trust**. That's repeated experiences of doing your job well. So every meeting you have, how you handle yourself as a head coach, those players experience that. If you run very organized meetings, if you're on time, if you're very competent, you earn more trust from that player.

And the final one—and the hardest one to earn—is called **Connection Trust**. That's when the players and staff have repeated experiences of you showing them you care for them. That takes time. It's very hard to get, very easy to lose. I've had coaches lose trust with players, and once you lose trust with a player nowadays it's so hard to get it back. And usually one of two things happens: either that player leaves [the program] or the coach leaves. So that's why we've spent so much time teaching our coaching staff how to earn and keep trust.

JOHN CALIPARI: The issue I've had and that happens to me at times, is that players have a higher opinion of me than they should. They look at me and at times are intimidated. I'm like, how could you look at me and be intimidated? One: Look at me. And two: I'm all for you. How does that intimidate you? The forty-some guys that played for me and made it in the NBA, they came here and took what they wanted. Yeah, we were there for them. Yeah, we pushed them. And yeah, we made us all play together and share for one another. But sometimes that intimidation gets in the way of me even being able to do the job I'm capable of doing. Because again, you shouldn't be intimidated by me. Maybe someone else. But not me. They want to please me so bad it gets in the way. I have to grow that trust every day that *I'm* here to help *you* thrive.

PATTY GASSO: The word players used to use in our program was *trouble*—I don't want to get in *trouble*. And when I heard our players saying those things, I felt like, wow, now we're at a different level. I am the person who's going to get you in *trouble*. But it's not trouble, it's more working through things. That doesn't mean I won't discipline. But the word *trouble* made me feel like there's a separation between us. I'm the adult, and you're the kid. That kind of thing. So I wanted to find a way to meet the team a little more halfway, while also understanding I'm still your coach and I don't cross that line, and you don't cross that line. I don't talk to them about it. This is just me knowing what I have to do in order to create that trust. I want them to be comfortable. And not all of them are still, because they've been trained in their lifetime to be, maybe, afraid of a coach. I don't want them to be afraid. I want them to trust me. I want them to know that I have their best interests at heart.

JIMBO FISHER: I always say this: The hardest person to trust is yourself—because you can't blame anyone else. With somebody else, you can say to yourself, well, I trusted him and he let me down. Can't say that about yourself. I tell players every day, when you can trust yourself is when you finally become a great player.

MACK BROWN: Trust is earned through action. An example is when I came back to coach at UNC, I sat down with every player and I said, "Why are you losing? Why isn't this working? Why aren't you over in the football building more? Why aren't you over in the players' lounge?" [They say,] "Well, Coach, the food is awful." Tell me why. I don't need to know the food is awful, I need to know specifically what part of the food is awful so I can fix the food. So Sally [Brown's wife] and I started eating breakfast, lunch, and dinner with those players every single day we were in town. And I would have them come up and tell me, "Coach, this food is too dry. This lettuce is old." And I said, "I gotcha. I'm with you." And I'd go back to the manager and say, "This is unacceptable. We're paying a lot of money for these meals, I want the meals better." The players notice you've taken what they've said and acted upon it. That builds their trust in you. Then we walked in the players' lounge and I gave all the kids a pad and pencil. "You said there aren't things in here that you like in the players' lounge." I said, "Tell me what you want." They said, "What do you mean?" I said, "You write down for me what activities or amenities you want in this room. You tell me what you want and we're going to do it." They said, "We want two pop-a-shots." I said, "Fine. Get on Google and tell me which two pop-a-shots you want. I want to know exactly what you want." "Coach, our lockers are bad. They get on us about the lockers being dirty, but we don't have any way to clean the lockers. They're wet and damp." I said, "Got it." So I brought the top locker company in the country in. And I had them bring their best lockers, like the ones they had installed at Texas, that they had used at Clemson, and LSU and Alabama. Best of the very best. And I said, "You guys come in and tell me what you'd like differently about this locker room." That was the buy-in process. Again, that shows I listened to their concerns and acted upon them to improve their experience. That builds trust.

So I said, "Okay, you got a new players' lounge, got a new locker room. I want it clean. I want it clean every day." Because I've now built equity in trust, they'll listen to your directives better. The players ask me, "Why do we have to clean our lockers every single day, Coach?" "Because we had more penalties than anybody else in the Atlantic Coast Conference. That's because we have no discipline. You have nice stuff now. So you're gonna take care of it." So, then a couple of them would leave stuff out, and I'd run the hell out of them. "I want it clean, men." Then a couple of them didn't have it clean and I said, "I'm gonna fire the equipment manager. If you're not willing to hold up your end of the relationship, someone else will have to pay for your decision." And they said, "No, Coach! Man, that's harsh!" I said, "Nope. It's called facts. It's called real life. I told you to keep it clean or there would be consequences. So you're either gonna have it clean, or I'm gonna walk Sally in there, and there's a towel on the floor, I'm either running you off or the equipment manager, but we're gonna have a clean room. And somebody has to answer for it if we don't."

So that's the way you build trust and responsibility. They know that if I tell them I'm gonna run them if they don't have a clean locker room, and I don't run them, then I lose my credibility. And that credibility was built through the trust I earned by listening to them and following through on what I said I was going to do.

JOHN CALIPARI: I laugh all the time about "keeping it real." People all want you to keep it real until you keep it real with them! They'd rather you keep it real with somebody else.

ROY WILLIAMS: You have to show them. Don't talk it. Prove it. Here's an example: we lose on Friday night to Auburn. Come back on Saturday and I get [former North Carolina All-ACC guard] Coby White to come down to my office. I said, "What are your thoughts about the NBA?" He said, "Coach, I never planned to come here just for one year." And I laughed a little bit and said, "I appreciate that, son. And I know you didn't. But you're ready to go. You'll be a top ten pick in the draft. Your family is not hungry, but it's not easygoing for your family. You need to go to the NBA." He had lost his father the August before his senior year in high school, so he has a mom and a brother and a sister, and none of them have a money tree growing in their backyard.

So I told him, "You're ready right now. And in my opinion, you should go. So you not only have my blessing, but you have my council and my advice that you should go." I told him he'd be very successful, and told him the reasons why he would be successful. So he leaves my office, and I told him to go home and talk to his family. Call them. Get them on the phone and talk. He comes back the next day, and says, "Coach, I think the NBA is the best thing for me, and my family is so appreciative that you decided to tell me that." His mom comes out in an article a few days later, and says, "Coby didn't have any idea what he was going to do. But he met with Coach Williams, and Coach Williams made the decision so easy, because Coach Williams thought that's what was best for Coby as an individual. And the trust that we had in him made it the easiest decision we've had to make, by far." The way to build that trust is to be truthful. Truth and trust go together.

JOE GIBBS: With teams and people working together, and particularly in team sports like I've been involved in, the collective mind of the team, all those individuals, they're gonna figure you out *(laughing)*. They're going to know what you stand for, and you can't fool them. Sometimes I'd say something in front of the football team, and I thought, *Well, I'm sure that slid by them. I'm sure they didn't get that.* And later on, sure enough, it would come back up. So the collective mind is going to figure out if they can trust you, and if you stand behind what you say. If you do, that's how you build trust with a team.

URBAN MEYER: Until the team you lead realizes that you are vulnerable, not just some figurehead that's beyond reproach, it's very hard to get that trusting relationship. Once they see that you're vulnerable and human—*vulnerable* is a great word, but the word for me is *care*. Once they know you care, especially nowadays, that's the key.

JIMBO FISHER: Who can really trust themselves? I think it's a much lower number than you could truly know. But you do know when it happens. Definitely. You can see that light turn on. I can't give you a number of how many I've had. But I can tell you how I know when they've made that step and trust themselves: the answers to my questions that they give me; the questions they ask back to me and why they're asking them, and the actions they take as a result. Boom. The light is on.

MACK BROWN: You earn trust by telling people you're going to do something—and then doing it. No empty words. Leaders can't have empty words. A lot of times that means you have to stand up for what's right, not what's easy. One of our players overslept and missed practice. He's the best receiver we've got. Great player. I thought about it for a long time. I didn't let him practice the rest of the week, and I suspended him for the game. And I sat and told him and the entire team why I was suspending him for the game. He wanted to come and be on the sideline during the game. I said, "No, you've lost your right. Because I told you, you have to be at every practice on time, every meeting on time, every class, every time." He asked for a ticket for the game. I said, "No. Sit somewhere and watch it on TV. I don't want you around. You've lost your rights. You have to pay dues to be part of this team and this process. You lost that. You didn't care enough about us to wake up. So you're not part of that process." And then what I explained to the team was this: "I lost a player in 2001, in a truck accident. So my whole morning at practice [when the player overslept and missed practice] I was worried about where this player was. I was conditioned to think the worst: I thought he was dead. We couldn't find him. He wasn't answering his phone. So I went through a process that I was afraid he was dead. I called the police. I called his mom. And he didn't care enough to let us know that he'd just overslept." I told him, and the entire team, that story. And we went through that process of trust. I told them, "This time I wasn't going to put this decision on you players and the leadership committee—I'm making the decision that he lost his right to dress and play in the game." Because if I don't follow through on my words, as the CEO of our program, I have no credibility. That's a moment and a decision when I, as the leader, needed to handle it in order to build trust within the organization. Now I'll tell you, it was hard as hell. It was not an easy decision. But it was right.

URBAN MEYER: It's the exact same thing in corporate America. Companies or businesses that are all driven by money, that's a false trust. That's a pseudo hope or opportunity. Hope and opportunity are what every athlete wants. Really, it's what everybody wants. And if you don't have hope and opportunity you go to a false opportunity. What's that? That's the $10,000 bonus. But if there's hope and opportunity to grow, such as becoming an owner of the company, that's so much more valuable than a $10,000 bonus. The strong companies, it's not about that bonus. It's about that ownership. It's about opportunity in that company.

JOHN CALIPARI: John Wall [former Kentucky All-American point guard] said, "Coach Cal never promised me one thing. He didn't promise me I'd start. He promised me to push me and make me the best player I could be." I want players that when we push them, they can trust we're about them. If they don't think you care about them, you're very limited into how much you can coach and lead them. And how aggressive you can get. If they know you care about them, coach them like it's your own child. They'll respond.

ROY WILLIAMS: Trust is also treating everybody differently, as long as it's fair. I tell them, I will not treat you all the same. But I am going to treat you all fairly. If one guy comes in two minutes late for our first meeting of the year, and he's a senior and truthfully was late for a good reason, I can handle that. But I will say immediately to those freshmen, "Don't let that happen to you. You haven't built up any trust with me."

And I think over the years, the treatment we've given our guys, and the fact that we've given them the information that, no question, is not in the best interests of our team but in the best interest of their lives as people, shows them that we care about them as individuals. It's an old cliché, but it's a cliché because it's true—I wouldn't give any of my players advice I wouldn't give my own son.

MACK BROWN: If you're a leader, you'll have to make difficult decisions you might not see coming. During my first go-round at North Carolina, there was a protest over a Black Culture Center on campus. And Jesse Jackson and Spike Lee came in and asked the players to protest our game against Army. I'd just met [my wife] Sally. And they asked the kids to go protest the Friday night team meeting, and go over to the Smith Center and have a rally in protest, and then play or don't play in the game, but miss the Friday night meeting. So I went to our chancellor, Paul Hardin, and John Swofford, our AD at the time, and I said, "Guys, I'm asking your permission to let me walk into this team meeting on Thursday before the Army game and tell the kids that if you miss our Friday night meeting, and our Friday night meal, then not only are you not going to play in the game, but you're kicked off scholarship." And they both said, "Wow." That's the way I felt. You're either in or you're out. And what you do for this team is one thing. Your social preferences, political preferences, your idealism outside of this team is something else. And they both said okay. So I walk into the team meeting and I say, "Okay, guys, here's what I got: Sally and I are really going to help you with the Black Cultural Center. I promise you that I will make it happen. It's something you were promised, and it hasn't been done. But that's not part of this football team. There are some of you that care, and there are some of you that do not care. So I'm telling you this: If you do not go to Friday night dinner and Friday night meeting, then you're not going to play in the ball game, as well as you're going to be kicked off the team. I'm not going to keep you on scholarship."

And you could hear a pin drop. I mean, oh my God. I told Sally when I walked out of there, I said, "Yep, probably just lost my job." And I walk out and say, "There is no negotiation. None. I'll help you in any way I can. We'll raise that money. We'll help you build the center. But it's not part of this football team." I felt very strongly that I had to stick to my guns. Sometimes in this life to create the right energy as a leader you have to take chances. And that was one hell of a chance I took. And I walked out of there not knowing whether I had a job or not. It ended up where four captains came up to my office—Tommy Thigpen and Corey Holliday are on our staff today, and they were two of those captains. And they came upstairs, and they said, "Coach, can we see you?" I was sitting in my office. And I said, "Yeeeeep." They said, "Listen, you're totally right. Everybody was in agreement with you, and I promise you that it will not be mentioned in a football setting again." I said, "Well, good. So everybody's going [to the meeting] on Friday night?" And they said, "Yes, sir—and we'll beat Army. So don't you worry about that. Everybody's in. Everybody's gonna buy into everything you said. We've got a couple of things we want to ask you." I said, "That's fair." They said, "Number one, there's three guys that are hurt. They're not going to dress and they're not going to play, can they not only go to the rally, but can they speak for the Cultural Center, not for the football team?" I said, "Yes, that's fair." They said, "Number two, would you have somebody video it, and then on Sunday any players that have an interest in watching it and hearing what was said, could actually watch it?" I said, "Yes, that's fair." They said, "Coach, that's it. You said you'll raise the money. We believe you. And we're all in." That was a breakthrough moment. Those young men trusted Sally and me as leaders in their lives that we'd follow through. We asked them to sacrifice for the team, and they expected us to sacrifice for the students at that university. And then Sally and I were very instrumental in raising the money, and the Black Cultural Center sits right across from our office right now. That goes back to trust. That story has never been told publicly before. In fact, Jesse Jackson came in and looked at our media guide to see how many African American coaches I had on my staff. And I had more African American coaches than white coaches. And he said, "I got no problem with you, Coach, see ya later." I said, "I got you, bud." That all goes back to trust. It's all trust between coach and player. Tell them something, and follow through, no matter how hard it is to do.

URBAN MEYER: Trust is the most important attribute of leadership structure. My very strong opinion on that is, if you don't have trust, you're wasting your time. It's going to be hard to lead someone out of a room without trust. But once you get trust, you can move mountains.

Smith's Sideline Summary: Trust

- Trust is the most important aspect of every meaningful relationship.
- Trust is hard to build and easy to lose. What took years to cultivate can disintegrate with one poor decision. Intentional care is vital to trust maintenance.
- Leaders are human and at times will make mistakes that compromise trust. Therefore, consistent, intentional deposits in the trust bank are vital to achieve balance.
- Trust is a teach-and-sow principle, not a preach-and-go principle.
- Tell the truth and follow through on the truth. Do it every time. And explain and care why you're doing it.
- Trust requires intimate time, boundless energy, and unwavering follow-through to produce. It is a seven-course sit-down dinner, not a grab 'n' go drive-thru window.

Chapter 3

COMMUNICATION + LISTENING

"Nothing in life is more important than that ability to communicate effectively."

—Gerald R. Ford, 38th President of the United States

What leaders say, and how they say it, has never been more critical. Because, as Tom Izzo stated in the "Leadership" chapter, communication today is not just *what* leaders instruct, it's the explanation of *why* a particular directive is issued. Consistent repetition of key messaging is essential to cut through the constant clutter we all navigate. We are inundated with an unprecedented volume of influential inputs via social media, mobile devices, television, and a hundred other ways. And not all of them are positive or productive. Distraction and unproductive time-sucks are limitless.

Without intentional messaging regarding direction, goals, culture, conviction, expectation, and execution, success is fleeting if not impossible. And without proper communication, success is most certainly not sustainable.

Clear, vulnerable communication informs and motivates people. Motivated people are productive people. Lack of consistent communication can result in folks feeling disconnected and listless. Listlessness results in complacency. Complacency signals doom.

One key aspect of productive communication is ensuring it's reciprocal. Listening is paramount to leading. Because clear messaging and open ears empower others. In my experience, few leadership traits are more empowering to a player or to an employee than feeling heard and seen by leadership.

When we are heard and seen, we do not question if we belong. We know we belong. Listening is proof of caring.

At the most basic human level, we yearn for belonging. Most of us want to be a part of something greater than ourselves. Even if our initial mission is selfish, the unity and satisfaction created within shared sacrifice is undeniable. To contribute individually to success collectively produces fulfillment. Effective leaders often communicate the power of shared sacrifice.

Complacency is something everyone with any level of success will battle. Success makes it easy to get comfortable. Communicating the evil of complacency is important in the quest to thwart it. If you see it, say it. Directly and clearly. Remind those you're leading that while they rest, someone else is working. Remind those you're leading that somewhere there is a Kobe Bryant dripping with sweat in a dimly lit gym at dawn while they're under the covers dreaming of the success he achieved. Remind them that if they don't attack practice and meetings and preparation with intention and intensity, they will get their ass handed to them by an opponent who does.

If you want to differentiate yourself in your environment, build a foundation at the intersection where your ability meets your opportunity. There is just one way: the right way. And most times, the right way is the hard way. Embrace the beauty within the barrier.

"Your ass has been preparing for this shit for fuckin' 365 days! I think about the fuckers in that locker room. I think about getting our opportunity! All the shit you went through this week to get ready for this game! Now is when you pay the fuckin' price! You go out there with energy, enthusiasm. Ain't nobody in this room should be cautious! Ain't nobody in this room should be nervous about shit! Go out here and FUCK THEIR ASS UP! Don't think about a scoreboard. Don't think about shit! You think about knocking the shit out of 'em! Did you hear what [the media] said on Monday? I sat in that fuckin' meeting! I wanted to go fuckin' play, RIGHT THEN! I'm damn proud of you, boys. You play the right way! You knock their ass off! You stay off the fuckin' ground! You tackle the fuckin' man with the ball! This shit's easy! Look at the right shit! Punish their ass on offense! And kick their ass on special teams, guys! It's about who the fuck WE ARE! I believe in you! Let's go!"

Ready to strap on a helmet and run through a brick wall? Those words were Kirby Smart's to his Georgia Bulldog football team during a pregame speech. Smart says he doesn't recall the exact game or opponent before which he delivered this verbal blowtorch. He says his pregame speeches all sound similar, and he has indeed issued quite a series of legendary motivational rants you'd be ill-advised to play aloud in Granny's living room. You may not love all the language choices. That message was issued in a locker room. A private, closed space. It was leaked to the public. And it gives a very direct example of the motivational tactics in the competitive arena. It ain't the boardroom or the corporate office. It's ball. Me? I *love* it. I *love* an old-fashioned, vein-popping, rowdy screaming motivational rant. It's like plugging your acoustic program into a hundred-watt amp.

The players are electrified by the intensity within the messaging.

In this example, Smart's messaging to his team is crystal clear: When you've prepared properly—which we know we have—the game-day mission is fundamental. We're tougher than they are, better than they are, and hungrier than they are. **Go kick their ass.**

The message to his team is intentional: We've prepared properly and today is *why* we've worked so hard, so go fly around that football field, play freely and without anxiety, and most important, have fun. **And go kick their ass.**

The message to his team is intense: The other team wants none of our smoke. **Go kick their ass.**

The message to his team was delivered with distinct purpose: We're the best team in this stadium today. We're the best team in this *country* today. But there are naysayers who doubt us. And those guys stand in our way. Let's go prove them all wrong. **Go kick their ass.**

Smart is an elite communicator and motivator. He works very hard at it and is intentional about it. His rant is like simple sugar in a jelly bean: It creates an instant and potent burst of energy. But it is not delivered for long-term impact. Long-term impact comes from consistent daily messaging, which is more like the carbohydrates in oatmeal: lessons that produce lasting, sustainable energy.

In the days leading up to each game, Smart is deliberate with key words and phrases designed to reach his players at their emotional level, while setting expectation and prompting deeper thought and conversation with meaning and truth. Here are some of Smart's phrases:

"Success comes to those who are too busy to be looking for it."

"Connection! Connection! Connection: 1 + 1 = 3!"

"Keep chopping wood."

"We will not be hunted at the University of Georgia. I can promise you that. The hunting we do will be from us going the other direction. We're not going to sit back and be passive."

"It's about us. That's all we got. And that's all we need."

"Burn the boats and take their boats. You either win or you die."

Countless coaches use key phrasing. In that way, Smart is not unique. I just have better understanding of his communication philosophy than some others, because I once did a feature piece for ESPN and the SEC Network that focused specifically on Smart's messaging. He told me he finds these phrases by reading and studying, and by consulting motivational experts. He says these weekly mantras are vital to his program, because when the goal is the same every year—to win the Southeastern Conference Championship and the National Championship—he as a leader must develop creative messaging that motivates and educates. Otherwise, it becomes white noise to the players that doesn't resonate as intended.

And there's another priceless layer, here, which multiple coaches mentioned in the "Leadership" chapter: time spent with players. To illustrate the power of time, I want to steal a passage from my previous book, *Never Settle*:

> Time is the rarest resource. While the drop of rain and the morsel of food cycle through its prism—returning again and again in alternate forms—time itself cannot be manufactured, re-created, retained, or corralled. Every tick of the clock is a moment then a memory... And as long days become short years, the memories of our moments flicker in a filmstrip of snapshots, providing an emotional bridge from what is to what was. No matter how much time we have, we always want more.

Kirby Smart is one of many elite coaches who are keenly aware that time spent with players, investing in *who* they are beyond *what* they are, is critical to reaching them emotionally. And reaching them emotionally helps drive home key messaging on a personal level, beyond merely a functional level. They not only take it into the competitive arena on Saturdays, they take it with them the rest of their lives.

These phrases may seem simple, and countless coaches use similar mantras every day. But when repeated over and over, they reach people and teach people in a profound way.

KIRBY SMART: The message can get lost in the delivery. So clear, direct communication is critical for every leader. I know a lot of really smart people who give me ideas and messages, who might not be able to deliver the messages. And I might not be able to come up with the right message all the time. But the combination of the message—and the delivery of the message—is critical. And I do think that the strongpoint of great leaders is communication of a clear message. What is a clear message? It's usually short. It's usually direct to the point. And it's driven home and reiterated and repeated enough that it sticks. It is ingrained in the people you're leading.

DABO SWINNEY: Communication is critical. If you're gonna lead people and get them to follow you, first you have to have a great vision. But you can't just have the vision. You've got to be able to articulate and communicate the vision with great clarity, in a way that motivates and inspires people, and gets them to completely buy in.

MACK BROWN: We start with communication. Because until you can get your players and your staff to talk to you and communicate with you, you've got nothing. And men don't communicate very well. Ladies talk all the time. Guys will talk a little bit about sports, they'll talk about the girl they like, they'll tell a joke. But we're not going to talk about serious topics to each other. That's just who we are. So communication is priority one. Let's get so we can talk to each other. Let's have a dialogue. That's very important. Secondly, back to trust and respect for a moment, those come from communication. So if I've built trust and respect, *and* I've got them talking to me, then I'm gonna find out what they really think. And now, I'm cooking with gas. Because now I know if they're on target with me. And if they're not, and it's becoming a problem, I got all that down. Without communication, it's over before it starts.

DOC RIVERS: Chuck Daly [1994 Naismith Memorial Basketball Hall of Fame inductee, two-time NBA Champion Detroit Pistons head coach] was one of the greatest communicators ever. In the year and a half before he passed away, we were talking. And I asked him if he could do his career over again, what would he do? And he said, I would communicate more. Basically saying, you can't communicate enough. You can't touch enough. You can't connect enough. I thought that was a fascinating answer from him.

PATTY GASSO: It's so interesting how communication has evolved over the years. My messaging is much different today than it was ten, twenty, thirty years ago. Messaging today, for me, is very much about wellness, happiness, peace. Maybe not even happiness, because happiness is short-lived. But the word *joy* is so important. I want them to love what they're doing. And these days, where the stakes are different, they're higher, social media has caused disruption in athletes, in their mindsets and the way they feel about themselves. So I feel like I'm constantly trying to just hammer home to them that they're good enough. They're loved. That mistakes are necessary to learn. That softball isn't an end-all, be-all. That softball and winning championships is not exactly what life is about. I think in this day and age, athletes are caught in their identity being related to the position they play, and what they do on the field. And that has caused a lot of disruption in sport, in general, and in the softball world where kids are quitting or taking drastic measures. It's tragic. And I don't want to leave this sport knowing that I'm not doing justice. I have to constantly change to the way the world is changing. And ten years ago to now is completely different, so I can't live ten years ago. I have to change with these athletes and change with the times, and right now the way I speak to them has to be about fulfillment, joy, and self-confidence.

TOM IZZO: The greatest threat to excellence is complacency. Nick Saban says that all the time, and he's exactly right.

Complacency is evil. That, and players listening to too many people. There are so many people out there now. You look at the level we're at in football and basketball, and you have so many people who want to make money off of your guys. I don't want to make any money off my guys. I got enough money. I want to do this for them. They need to know that, and you have to communicate it very directly and consistently so they hear you and know that what you're communicating is gospel.

FRANK BEAMER: Say what you mean and mean what you say. Be exact in what you say. And always follow through. If you say it, carry it through, whether that's consequences or instruction. If you don't follow through, your words are empty.

JOE GIBBS: People learn one of three ways: First, they learn by hearing it, so you need to effectively communicate the message. Because for some people, that's the way they'll learn and incorporate the lesson you're trying to get across. The second way is by seeing it. So if you have a game plan or an overhead [visual], make sure that it's understandable. And third, we know that some people learn by doing it. Show them how. You need to be a good teacher. Good leaders approach it that way: from a teaching standpoint.

JIMBO FISHER: You can see it when it clicks, when the message you've been consistently trying to deliver gets delivered, and what you're telling the player registers. That's fun.

ROY WILLIAMS: Michael Jordan taught me a lot about the value of clearly communicating a message, and then listening to how the player responds. It's a long story, so bear with me: In Michael's senior year of high school, they lost, I think, seven games. They didn't make the state tournament. And they had a six-ten kid on his team who went to UNC Charlotte. So they had a quality team. In my second year [as an assistant coach at North Carolina], I made a fateful mistake that was special for me in my own education: I suggested to Coach [Dean] Smith that we should have a very demanding preseason conditioning program. And as a young coach, that tells you this: If you suggest something, you better be prepared to follow through and enforce it. So Michael shows up here at Carolina, and I tried to bury those boys with this program. Monday, Wednesday, Friday, three days a week for four weeks, I tried to *bury* their asses. I wanted somebody puking, or I didn't think we'd done enough. Now this wasn't me having a Napoleonic complex, trying to make them admire me, respect me, hate me all at once. It was that I wanted us in better shape than anybody in the country. And I thought the toughness we'd get from that would be very good. So early on in Michael's freshman year, first or second week of this conditioning program, he comes to me and says, "I want to be the best player who's ever played at North Carolina." And I said, "Well, son, you've got to work harder. Because you didn't work very hard in high school." And he said, "I worked as hard as everybody else!" And I said, "Oh, well excuse me... I thought you just told me you wanted to be the *greatest player who every played the University of*

North Carolina. Son, that's a hell of a list. You have no chance. Because if your attitude is, *I'm gonna work as hard as everybody else,* you have absolutely no chance to be the best player ever here. None." I told him straight up. Although I didn't consider it at the time, I communicated directly to him what he had to do to reach his personal goal. I did not mince words. He took it from there—boy, did he ever.

DOC RIVERS: To make sure the messaging I want conveyed to my team is successful, it has to come from me, it has to come from my coaches, it has to come from everybody in the organization. We all have to speak the same language. And when they hear it over and over and over again, it can get through. You can't have weak links in your organization that say, "Well, what I would do is…" You have to coach your coaches. You have to coach your staff. Do you know who touches the players the most? The trainers! Equipment managers! Strength staff! So you have to coach them on the messaging.

TOM IZZO: There's so many people in their ear telling players what they *want* to hear, instead of what they *need* to hear—and what they *need* to hear ain't always nice. It's got to be direct and honest. It's got to be real. They hear from people who don't always have their best interest in mind, or truly have any knowledge. I put in more than thirty-five years in this profession to try to get where I am, so I got resources. I can call NBA GMs and owners, I can call Nick Saban and ask him how to win a championship, or Urban Meyer. I got all the resources in the world to help you, and you're going to listen to a guy because he says he's a street agent? I think complacency and who you're listening to are huge threats—the biggest threats. Keep your circle small. Your circle has to be really small. And as a leader, you better communicate that to your personnel very directly.

GREG SANKEY: We've set communication parameters on our own expectations in the SEC office. I think you have to be intentional about the how. Because you can't spend all your time on the phone or in meetings, so you have to prioritize the who.

KIRBY SMART: When the goal is to convey a specific message, a leader can't focus on a bunch of different things. You can't have a bunch of different points. You've got to be clear, concise and to the point, and drive your message home in the way you deliver it. And I do believe that's part of our success in messaging at the University of Georgia: the people providing us those messages, who are kind of like a songwriter, and I'm the singer—the songwriter creates the words and the messaging, and the singer delivers that message. I wouldn't be a very good messenger if I didn't have great songwriters. And I think the people behind the message, who create those, have been a huge asset to me as leader.

NANCY LIEBERMAN: Clear communication is everything. Without it, you can't establish expectations or lead others to achieve their potential. [2008 Naismith Memorial Basketball Hall of Fame inductee, five-time NBA Champion coach] Pat Riley said to me one day, "Nancy, I'm not a mind reader. You have to tell people what you want and what you need." That's the best piece of advice I've ever received. A light went on for me. It was amazing! Say what you want. I wanted to be in the NBA one day. A true communicator is clear and concise, and the same message has to be delivered over and over and over again. That's what creates true accountability, and people believe in you as a leader.

MACK BROWN: I have a leadership committee, and our team makes a lot of our decisions, or suggestions to me, and then I make the final decision. The same with our staff. I ask everybody on our staff what they think. Communicate. Some people feel like that's a waste of time. But from my standpoint, I need to know what they think, so if I don't go in their direction, I know I may have some work to do to have them buy in. I've always felt like you can take a bad idea with ordinary people, and if everybody works together you can still make it work. But if you take a great idea, and not everybody is bought-in? You'll fail. So I'm all about being all-inclusive. I need everybody in the football family to buy in and know that these things are going to work and feel like it's the best thing to do. And that begins with clear communication, and open ears to listen to what their opinions are.

NANCY LIEBERMAN: Another important aspect of communication that extends to life, love, business, sports, is the Cs: Be clear, concise, concrete with your messaging, be correct, be coherent, be complete, but also be courteous. It is three-sixty communication. People want to be heard, especially in this generation. So, if my assistant coaches know that I value their thoughts, it empowers them. Whether I use their opinions or not in the head coach seat, it's important that the people who work for me, or play for me, know that I value what they have to say. Do not get mad at me if I don't use that play that you gave me, but I want you to know that I 100 percent have a belief system that you've done your work. Three-sixty communication is paramount to communication being effective.

FRANK BEAMER: I touched on this earlier, but it's critically important in the communication aspect of leadership: Never embarrass someone in front of their peers. If you do, a lot of times they'll react differently because they're trying to defend themselves. If I ever had a serious problem with a player or coach, I called them into my office and discussed it one-on-one, look each other in the eye, and told them exactly what I thought was wrong. In those instances, I found that communicating individually is more effective. If it's important enough, meet privately about it and work through solutions.

ROY WILLIAMS: Listening is one of the most important aspects of leadership because if you're listening, you don't assume.

DOC RIVERS: There's never been a great leader who is not a great listener.

KIRBY SMART: Leadership *starts* with being a good listener. Sometimes people put it in reverse order. But to be a good leader you've got to listen to people. You've got to know their perspective and know how to consider and manage those unique perspectives and situations. Good listening is the key to any leadership status, because everyone wants to be heard and understood, and you cannot hear or understand without intently listening.

TIM CORBIN: I don't know that there's a skill that matters more, or is more important, than listening. The power of listening may be as important a communication trait as you can have as a leader. Because without it, you're not learning. Genuine listening is the ability to listen with the intent of putting yourself in someone else's shoes, to try to get on their wavelength, to listen to their frame of reference. And it's listening to what's being said—and what's *not* being said—so you can really take in the message and have the ability to properly respond or not respond. It opens up a lane of clarity. Because when you're really listening, then you're not thinking so much about what you're about to say. You're listening to the message so you can properly respond, if, in fact, you need to. To me, that's true communication.

FRANK BEAMER: Listening is critical. If you're talking before you listen, then you may lead a player, or your team, down the wrong path. Listening allows you to know exactly what the concern is, or the necessary direction is. And if you listen before you talk, then you can communicate an answer that points the right direction. Listening is a fantastic skill.

JIMBO FISHER: *(laughs)* It's *critical*. In recruiting, if you listen to them, they'll *tell* you how to recruit them. If you listen, in certain areas, you can see and understand how a guy thinks. And you need that before you can communicate with him on an individual, personal level. And the only way you can do that is watch his actions, listen to his words. And when I say listening, to me, it's not really just listening to words, it's also paying close attention to actions.

DOC RIVERS: I think leaders listen more than they lead. You have to. You have to hear what your players are saying. You have to understand what they're saying. You have to have the feeling of your players. And within that, leadership is also not a popular position. I have to listen to my players. I have to listen to my coaches. But there's times I have to be the only one that disagrees.

ROY WILLIAMS: If you listen, you learn. Coach [John] Wooden always had a great concept that nobody ever learned anything by talking. And I told him one time that I really liked that lesson. I told him, "I talk too much, myself." And he said, "Yeah, but I've watched you at practice, I've watched you in games, and you listen, also." You *have to* listen to them.

LEONARD HAMILTON: I read body language, facial expressions, tone of voice when I'm communicating with my guys. Awareness. I'm always aware! I believe it's sacrilegious to worry. Because if you've given all you have with the ability that God has blessed you with—if you're not letting anyone out-work you, you're not making excuses, you're thinking before you speak—there is no reason to worry. I don't have highs, I don't have lows. I'm always on point. And the more stressful the situation becomes the more aware I am. You develop those skills when you're walking home at night, when you're always on that edge. You walk it, you talk it, you live it. And you share those experiences with the guys you're leading. I've been in environments where I'm the only Black guy there. Now, I've had a few moments where I've taken a step back. One time I called my mother when I'd just gotten to school [at the University of Tennessee at Martin] and I said, "Mom...some of these people might be prejudiced." And she said, "Where you goin', baby?" That's all she said: "Where you goin'?" I said, "I don't know if I can stay here, Mom." She said, "Why?" I said, "These people here might be a little bit prejudiced." "So where you goin' then?" It was like she reached through the phone and said, *Fool, come on! We didn't raise you that way. Deal with it.* So my point is this: All my leadership skills come from my instincts of survival and trying to overcome obstacles, and I'm extremely sensitive to me trying to coach and teach and develop.

TOM IZZO: Listening is what I've learned. Listening is a great art. I have a saying around here that I use in my camps: Learn to listen; listen to learn. A lot of people will learn to listen, but they aren't really listening to learn anything. That includes me, by the way. I think sometimes when you get to be a dictator: a head coach, a principal, CEO or leader of a company, whatever you want to call guys that have a lot of people under them, we do more talking than listening. The great, great leaders do more listening than talking. And I had to learn that. I'm not alone.

TIM CORBIN: Not to get too flowery here, but listening is really a way to show someone how much you care about them and how much you love them. A breakdown in any relationship is a lack of communication. And a true breakdown of any relationship is the ability for it to be one-sided, [in which] one person does the communication and the other person listens—but it doesn't go back and forth. So it's not reciprocal. You eliminate conflict by listening. And then when you have a group of people that listen very well, you find out listening becomes contagious. And it can transform relationships.

NANCY LIEBERMAN: You can either fuel somebody with your words, or you can break somebody down with your words. It's the legend of the sun and the wind. They got into an argument over which one was stronger. And then a traveler came down the road and they decided to settle it by seeing who could force him to take off his coat. So the sun hid behind the cloud, and the wind just blasted him, which made the guy wrap himself in his coat even more tightly. And then the sun came out with its gentle, caressing warmth, and put heat on him, and he was forced to take his coat off. Think about that. Angry words make others withdraw, shrivel or shut down, especially if they're insecure. Angry words confirm their worst fears and opinions about themselves. But gracious words help them to open up, discover what's good about themselves, and motivate them to reach higher. We've seen that before on the field and in the office. Someone is getting yelled at, being demeaned, and they don't know how to handle it. And that's part of leadership. If you only have one tool in your toolbox, and it's a hammer, you're not going to get the response you're looking for. And we just have to make sure that we're aware of the people, and we know we can course-correct if you know we're a little too aggressive with people. And I find that with my players also. Players and teams and companies and people go through struggles. The question is, how will they respond? That's part of the development of the people you work to lead.

JOHN CALIPARI: I say this every year—for a basketball team to truly reach its potential, they have to be empowered. It has to be *their* team. They have to be able to say, "Coach, let's go for an hour today." When they're empowered—and it's not because they're lazy, it's because they need the time off. When they're empowered, you listen. That's when you know you've reached them.

TOM IZZO: We played Syracuse and Iowa State in Detroit [in the 2000 NCAA Tournament]. We were down at halftime in both games. So the first game, we're down fourteen points at halftime against Syracuse. I come walking down this long hallway, and I said, "Man, my personality is go in there and tear them up." But then I thought, *Man, we're shaken. We're down.* So I was kind of leaning toward building them up in that speech. But I walk into the locker room, and Mateen Cleaves has his best friend since fourth grade grabbed up by the shirt in a locker, and he's yelling at Morris Peterson, "You're playing awful! You've got to be better!" And I walk in, and everybody turns and looks at me. I said, "Hey, don't let me stop you." And I grabbed a chair and sat down and said, "Just continue with what you're doing." You talk about an empowered team! The media asked me after what I said to my team at halftime. I joked with them that I really gave it to the team. I'll be honest, I spoke for about two minutes. Cleaves handled it. Cleaves addressed my team. After four years together, I had a relationship with him that was so strong, *he* was delivering *my* message. And when that message is coming from one of your own [peers] it's a lot better than coming from the coach or dictator or company president. As a leader that's important, that each year somebody in that [player] uniform is delivering my message.

KIM MULKEY: You have to let them have some ownership at some point. But you don't give that ownership to them until you've been around each other for a while and you make them understand, *I'm just the leader.* That's it. This is *your* team. *You* own it. As the leader, I'm gonna guide you and direct you as best I can. But I'm not going to do it for you.

ROY WILLIAMS: A leader who listens helps everyone in the organization feel empowered in the decision-making process.

JOHN CALIPARI: When we're in the huddle, there are times I say, "Should we go zone, here? What do you guys think?" It empowers them to make choices. So they walk in the huddle and say to me, "Let's do *x, y, z,* here on this play, Coach. Let's go to so-and-so." I'll always do it because it takes it off my plate and puts it on their plate. And that means we're one step closer to being an empowered team. [In 2019–2020,] we became empowered when I got thrown out of the game at Arkansas [January 18, 2020]. And [former Kentucky point guard] Ashton Hagans put his arm around me as I walked off the court and said, "Coach, we got this. We're good." And I walked in and suddenly they're off and running. They win that game. My staff did an unbelievable job. But those players were empowered. They said they were talking in every huddle, talking to each other, and relying less on me and more on each other. *That* is when you've achieved your best leadership. It's when they become empowered, and it's not your team anymore. It's *their* team. And you've then done your job, because you've gotten to reach beyond where they thought possible, and they now believe. It is their team now.

TOM IZZO: I've had to try to change even who I am. I just saw a quote from [former Michigan State All Big Ten guard] Gary Harris, "I was so sick of the meetings and film sessions [at Michigan State], until I got to the NBA and didn't have them anymore. Then I missed them." That is a big key. You have to have meetings, and in those meetings you have to spend time with your guys. I always tell my guys here, don't take them into your office to talk to them. Take them to lunch. Walk with them across campus to class. Take them out to your house. Sit in your basement and watch a game. Because going into the coach's office is like going to the principal's office—the only time you do it is when something's wrong! Do it outside. If you want to talk to a guy heart-to-heart, and actually get anywhere with it, get out of the office. Because I always felt, if I got called to "The Office" my ass was in trouble. Once they feel they're on your turf, they're less apt to tell you how they're truly feeling, less apt to be an open communicator. It can be intimidating. And I want the truth. So I do want to listen. I've acquired that and become better at that, but it's a difficult task. Because people perceive that when you're the leader, the coach, the captain, you're always supposed to have all the answers. A lot of times, the answers lives in the person you're talking to. Not in yourself.

ROY WILLIAMS: It's not the old school way: my way or the highway. That's not reality. In reality, the old-school guys like to *say* that's what they did—my way or the highway. But that's not what they did. The great leaders always listened.

TIM CORBIN: One thing athletes want to see in their teachers and their coaches—someone who's real, someone who's a human being, someone who's just like them and has the same experience as them to some degree; he or she doesn't set themselves apart because they're like the Wizard of Oz, behind a curtain, so you can never really see them or understand them. Vulnerability allows a student athlete and coach to know one another because they find a lane of communication.

PATTY GASSO: Listening is so powerful. And it's ego-driven, as well. Can a coach—who likes to talk a lot—sit there and listen and let them talk, and ask questions that will encourage them to talk more? That's communication. Versus, let me tell you how to fix it! This is their journey. I'm a guide. This is them reflecting on what they're experiencing. And the more

I'm involved in trying to fix it, the more they would resent me in the end. College softball turns girls into women. That's what it is. It's making them understand what they need, and how to get it. I'm there to aid them. And to aid them I have to listen to them.

TOM IZZO: If you talk to twenty coaches, I bet you nineteen will tell you they don't deal with the parents. I do. As part of our midnight madness, parents have to come in and I go over everything from legal issues to grade issues. And I do it with them all in the same room. That gives me the ability to say, "What do you want me to do if your kid tests positive for drugs?" Well in front of everybody else they'll say, "You have to suspend them!" What do you want me to do if your kid's not going to class? And I make them answer in front of everybody. It's been one of the coolest and most effective things I've done every year. Because if a kid is unhappy, the first person they're calling is their parents, right? And if I have the parents on my side, I've won half the battle already. [Former Michigan State All-American] Mateen Cleaves's mother, and Morris Peterson and those early guys I had, their parents told me, "Coach, you do whatever you got to do. I'm backing you 100 percent." It's not the same now. You have to win parents and kids over. Back then, my championship title won them over. Head Coach. Back then the title won them. Not now. Now, titles don't win you people. It's your relationship that wins you over. So I try to do both with parents and with student athletes. Because to accomplish what we want to accomplish, I have to communicate clearly and have everybody on my side.

ROY WILLIAMS: Two days after that conversation with Michael, where he tells me he wants to be the greatest Tar Heel ever, we're back up there on the track. This is in September. And Michael walks by and says, "I want to talk to you at the end of this." We did the workout, and at the end several people, myself included, are sitting around on the grass. And eventually it's just me and Michael. And he said, "I'll remember what you said." He said, "Coach, I've done a lot of thinking, and I want you to know, right now, you'll never see anybody work harder than me." I said, "Okay, great. Show me." So now we've begun communicating at a deeper level. He listened to me. And I listened to him and gave him direction. And his freshman year, eyes wide open, ears wide open, everything we asked him to do, he tried to kill it. He wanted to kill everybody. And he got better and better, so now he's getting more confident. And then he hits the jump shot to beat Georgetown and win the [1982 NCAA] national championship.

So now he's very confident. And he comes back to school as a sophomore, grew from six four and a half to six six, his vertical jump was better, and there was an unbelievable increase in his speed in the forty-yard dash. The day before we started practice we did all of our testing—vertical jump, standing reach, height, weight. But we did the forty-yard dash. Freshman year he ran a 4.5. That's pretty good. His sophomore year, it's me, Coach [Bill] Guthridge, and

Mark Davis, our trainer. All three of us have stopwatches. We're not professional timers. But we timed him, and I looked at my watch and it said 4.38. And I said, "Coach Guthridge, what time did you get?" He turned to Mark and asked him what time he got. None of us would say what we clocked Michael at. Mark said, "I had 4.39." I said, "Michael, I need you to run that one more time." And that sucker, as he walked past me—I'll never forget this—he looked at me and grinned and says, "Faster than you thought, huh, Coach?" He goes and runs the forty again. Blow the whistle, we got three guys who are not professional timers, and he goes flying by us. I say, quietly, "4.37." And Coach Guthridge said 4.38 and Mark said 4.38. So, he'd gained an inch-and-a-half height, was jumping higher, running faster, and had that confidence from seeing the benefits of all the hard work the year before. Plus, he's made the shot to win the national championship, and was the defensive player of the game in the national championship! He dominated everything in his path after that. And every single day he dominated, he got better, and he wanted to dominate more. The difference in Michael Jordan is that he had it inside of him— but he needed me to honestly communicate to him how hard he had to work to bring it out of himself. He took pride in saying, and doing, that "nobody's going to outwork me." Point is, you don't coach everyone the same, and you don't communicate to everyone the same. With Michael Jordan, you told the man one time and he handled it from there. If you challenged Michael verbally, as I did in that instance, hold on tight because he's going to try to kill you. Not everyone is wired like that.

JOHN CALIPARI: Public communication can have a personal impact, meaning the players are listening to what you say to the world. The way you deliver those words is important. I think when we win, I make sure I give credit to every single person on this team. And when we lose, I take responsibility. And I tell them that, and I'm gonna do it. If we lose a game, you'll know it, I'll put the loss on myself. And I want them to know it's okay to be wrong. It's okay to take responsibility when things go bad. Because I think you get closer with your team and they'll fight more for you. They'll play more aggressively because they know, if it doesn't work, you'll have their back. So I think it's important in leadership. The victory is everybody's. The failure? It's yours. You take it on. This one is on me. And you communicate that message loudly and directly to the world.

TOM IZZO: I had a kid whose dad played a little basketball. The kid was a good player but rough around the edges and kind of lazy, not really self-motivated. So his dad called me and says, "Why isn't [my son] doing a little more?" I said, "Why don't you come up to practice? Come on up here and watch." He goes, "You'll let me come watch?" I said, "Hell yeah, come on!" So he comes up for two days and watches us practice. And I tell him, "Now, after practice we're going to sit in my film room and we're going to watch film on the practice. You played small college ball. Then we're going to get [your son]." Well, it wasn't twenty minutes into the film session, he turns to [his son] and goes, "Why you loafing up and down the court?" They see it differently when you present it. It's right there. Look at it. So that little bit of time I spend with them pays great dividends. I have an academic advisor come in and talk to them. I have the chief of police come in and talk to them. I have lawyers come in and talk. I have all these people come in and talk as part of my one-hour session with the parents. And then when I say, "How do you want me to handle your kid?" And I don't always handle them like some want me to. But I'm giving them the option. And they normally come through with exactly how I feel. Because in front of everybody else, they're never going to say, "Hey, if my kid skips a whole bunch of classes I still want you to play them!" They won't say that! So when I get done with that, I always say, "Hey, I gotcha." Because I make them reiterate what I already believed.

JOHN CALIPARI: When I was at Memphis, we lost the [2008] national championship game. We're up nine points with 2:40 to go in the game, whatever it was. We miss five of six free throws to end the game. Five of six! Or we win the game! We were up nine! We make two out of six, we win the game. And we missed five of six. After the game I said, "Look, we had a nine-point lead with 2:40 to go, and that's on me as a head coach to win the game." That's what was communicated publicly. The players hear that. I never put it on the free throws. During my career, I've tried to be that guy, to let the guys know it's okay, to teach them that it's okay to be wrong. You have to verbalize that. You show them through action, but you also verbalize that you were wrong and you mean it. If I get on a guy, or I'm wrong about it, and it wasn't fair, I will apologize, and say I'm sorry. It is not always easy to say you're sorry. But if it's right, do it. Or I'll go kiss a kid on the forehead and say, "Look, I was wrong and I'm sorry I said what I said." I think it's important for them to see you that way, when you lead, that this guy is making it about me, he's taking responsibility when it goes bad, gives us credit when it goes well. If he's wrong, he'll say it. I've learned that taking that approach empowers people.

TOM IZZO: Communication is reciprocal. Again: Listening to their points of view gives them some ownership of the program. You don't have to do what they say. But every once in a while they'll come up with a good reason or explanation and I'll listen to them. We adjust. There's only one way to be great. That's to be disciplined and organized and be self-motivated. They've got to be evaluated. But I get those parents on board, it's tremendously beneficial. And presidents of companies? I'd have a family day. Some NFL teams do it. I'm big on those things. Getting the whole families involved. It's vital for me. It assures you're all on the same page from the very start.

URBAN MEYER: People often ask me how to handle a certain situation within a team. My first question back is, what kind of team am I dealing with? To go with the listening point, over the years I would always scan the back of the team room as the team would come in for the team meeting. And there's three types of teams to deal with: One is in there screwing around before the meeting starts, loud and obnoxious, saying things that aren't appropriate. That's the kind of team you don't want. So you have to go in there, dive right in the middle of it, maybe break them down a little bit. Then there's the team that's very quiet, to the point that you can tell maybe that they don't like each other and there's not much confidence. That's the kind of team you have to lift up. Then there's the team that's very businesslike, a gentle roar in the room, that's getting along but not overly obnoxious, not overconfident. That's the perfect team. So, you have to ask yourself, *What kind of team am I dealing with today?* The less you listen, the less you know that answer. I've made errors with that in the past. I'd go about it one direction, and that's not the kind of team I had. So, you have to listen.

TOM IZZO: There's three aspects of college. There's the athletic aspect if you're an athlete. There's the academic aspect and the social aspect. I always tell my players, pick two. But remember, nobody wants to pick academics, but you've got to be eligible! So your social life is going to take a back seat. Because if you scrimp on your athletic life, you ain't making it at this level. And if you don't put in the time academically, most kids aren't making it at this level. So the social life takes a back seat. I talk openly about that. I'm very honest with my guys. Sometimes that gets me in trouble. I tell them sometimes, "You're not good enough to go pro." "Well, Tom, Dick, and Harry over here say I am." "Well, here's why you're not." I've had guys who were good enough, and I got buddies in the NBA who I call and ask. I do my homework because I want to help you. Then I say, "Don't believe me? Let's call Magic. He was a GM. Steve Smith played in the league. Let's get some input from guys who know." I'm up front and real with my guys to a fault. Sometimes maybe too real.

ROY WILLIAMS: This doesn't speak directly to communication or listening, but if you'll indulge me here, I have to tell you one more story about Michael Jordan's will, and if your goal is to inspire people, it will resonate with them. Fast-forward to 1992, ten years after that initial conversation with Michael. [Former Kansas forward] Mark Randall is drafted to go play for the Chicago Bulls. He's their number one pick. So I tell Mark, "All right, son, I bet you $10 to the dollar, you'll get to training camp and the first week you'll call me and say, nobody works as hard as Michael Jordan." He said, "Coach, I'm a rookie. You think I'm going to let anybody outwork me?" I said, "Okay, ten to one." The third day of practice, Mark calls me and says, "Coach, the bet's off. I've never seen anything like this." And this was after Michael had been in the league for eight years! He's the MVP! Mark told me B. J. Armstrong had sprained his ankle, and they're playing five on five. End of the third day of practice. He said, "I turned around and grabbed one of those mesh shirts to put it on and run out there, and somebody pushed me out of the way and ran out on the court before I could get in. It was Michael Jordan!" He said, "Coach, this is the end of the third day of hard practices, some two-a-days. I'm a rookie trying to make it. And he knocks me out of the way so he could run in and they didn't have to stop running pick-up." It's that kind of thing. He had tremendous personality. Tremendous desire. And he got going himself. It wasn't anything anybody said. Now, it might have been something where I told him what I thought about what he'd done in the past. I communicated that to him and he heard it loud and clear. But he told me nobody would ever outwork him. And nobody did until the last day he played. He's the best I've ever seen as a basketball player. It's hard to compare centers, like Kareem or Chamberlain or Russell, to guards like Michael. But I think he's the greatest that ever played. And I think he'd be the greatest that ever played if he started today, because nobody has ever had better focus, desire, drive, and blessings. Tiger Woods is the only guy I've ever seen who had that same singular focus that Michael Jordan had.

Smith's Sideline Summary: Connection + Listening

- Clear, direct, honest communication is critical to successful leadership.
- Organizational trust and respect are derived from productive communication.
- Leaders must follow through on their words, whether they're for instruction or for discipline.
- Leaders must be intentional about communicating the how, and prioritize the who.
- Leaders listen more than they lead. If you listen, you do not assume. If you don't listen, you don't learn.
- People want to be heard. Listening to them empowers them.
- To ensure the message is delivered, everyone in the organization must speak the same language. That starts at the top.
- Leaders communicate praise to their team when they win and assume blame when they lose.
- Don't fuck with Michael Jordan.

AUTHOR'S NOTE: During my research for this project, an impactful philosophy regarding communication came from Georgetown University basketball coaching icon John Thompson, which I read in his tremendous autobiography, *I Came as a Shadow*:

There's a difference between communicating with a person and motivating a person. Communication is when someone understands what you are saying. Motivation is when they act on it.

Chapter 4

DELEGATION

"*Don't tell people how to do things. Tell them what to do, and let them surprise you with their results.*"

—George S. Patton, general, United States Army

One of the great challenges many self-driven individuals experience is delegating responsibility. When you've earned callused hands and a hardened psyche on the climb toward leadership positions, empowering others to help make decisions on your behalf could potentially impact the entire organization, and can be difficult.

When you're self-made, it's not easy to trust someone else to do it correctly. Here's the difference: Leadership often requires a macro perspective. To see the big picture. Leaders are forward-thinking and they have a broad scope. They play chess, not checkers. This is more binocular than microscopic. CEO-level leadership requires a long view, while empowering others to focus on the granular perspective.

And as an organization grows, leaders must empower their teams to take on more responsibility. Leaders beget leaders. For example, take a football head coach who was once an offensive coordinator, renowned for unique play concepts and schemes and strategic acumen. But as he ascends to head coach and CEO of his program, and more of his time each day is devoted to the countless responsibilities the head coach has—alumni functions, recruiting, broad scope macroplanning—he can spend less time in the nuance of specific game planning.

Yet, rather than delegate play-calling to his offensive coordinator—whom he obviously trusts enough to hold such a high-profile role—he continues calling the offensive plays during games. And because of the focus required to devise intricate game plans, he loses focus on the broad-scope perspective of the program, and the overall tenor of the program suffers. And eventually, so does performance and outcome.

This does not happen to everyone. There are coaches who excel in both roles. But there are also myriad examples of those who didn't and were stubborn to adjust. And the decline may not be immediate. It may take years to manifest.

The thinner a man gets stretched away from his center, the weaker he is on both sides.

Here's an analogy regarding my own career that I use sometimes. When I was kid, my momma, Joy, would drop my buddies and me off at the Pearisburg Town Pool with a dollar. Back then, in the mid-1980s, a dollar bought you a Fun Dip with the vanilla dipstick, two rounds on the Dig Dug video game console that shocked the absolute hell out of you when you used wet hands to drop in the quarter, and a chunky, meaty candy bar–size Laffy Taffy.

When we unwrapped that Laffy Taffy and took a big bite from the end, it was a chewy burst of flavor that lasted and left us fulfilled. But if we took that Laffy Taffy, one end in each hand and slowly pulled the ends apart, the center got thinner and thinner. And if we took a bite from that thin center that had been stretched so far, it was not chewy or meaty, did not last, was not nearly as flavorful, and was not remotely fulfilling.

Leaders can't afford to be stretched so thin that they lose their flavor, or outright disappear.

When we're good at something and it's always worked for us, we are conditioned to believe that we can work, plan, or coach our way out of a lull and back to excellence.

Are we secure enough to look in the mirror and know our stubbornness is impacting our company? In many cases, delegation is the answer. Delegation empowers others. Giving another person the responsibility to not just succeed but to excel is a statement: *I believe in you.*

The final decision belongs to the leader. Because the leader is ultimately responsible for success or failure. But delegation is self-confidence; micromanagement is insecurity.

TOM IZZO: The most important part of delegation is you have to be comfortable in your own skin. I always want to hire somebody who's better than me. Every hire. I know a lot of presidents of companies who want to hire people that they can put their thumb on and control. That's weakness. And it won't last long.

GREG SANKEY: There is, for high achievers, a confidence that *I know what I'm doing.* And if it can't get done right, I'll just do it myself. And that's a bit of a confession, if I'm being honest. We have an expectation of excellence, and if it's not met, there's an inclination of *Just let me do it.* So for me it took a while to say, *I have to trust the people around me to do the job at a very high level. I need to be able to communicate a level of expectation and then get out of their way.* And if you can't do that, then you either have to look at yourself or your expectations.

KIRBY SMART: Delegation is a delicate balance. It's an ever-changing balance. My first years as a head coach, I wasn't nearly the leader that I was capable of being, because I wasn't delegating enough. And as the years have come and gone, I definitely delegate more, and I pick and choose where I'm trying to reiterate a point or make a point. Number one, it gives your staff better morale. Number two, it rewards them to be original, and you don't beat down new ideas and new thoughts and new energy, because that usually affects morale. If you want morale to be good, you better allow for creativity among your staff. And I really think that's an area I've grown, to say, *Okay, let's try it his way. Maybe it fails and he takes value in that. Maybe we try it and it works and it's better, and we adopt it as our own.* Those things have made me a much more patient coach and leader, not to mention much easier to work for.

JIMBO FISHER: The challenge with delegation is knowing that the person you're giving responsibility is actually getting all the important details across to your players or staff. You can delegate and get generalities. Do they truly understand the precision of everything you're trying to get across? That's where coaches and businesspeople have a hard time. It's not that you don't believe in them. It's just the little nuances that allow you to coach different people differently, and making sure each coach truly understands that guy.

ROY WILLIAMS: I grew up under [Naismith Memorial Basketball Hall of Fame North Carolina head coach] Dean Smith. Practice was very, *very* dominated by Coach Smith. And I did it the same way, but I also made sure that there were always times during a practice, or individual workouts, that my coaches were in charge of things. That ensures they're seen as coaches in the players' eyes, not just *my assistant coaches.* There's a big distinction there.

NICK SABAN: I hear every play that's called. I hear every defense that's called. And I have the right to veto every one of those things. So, do I think [offensive and defensive] coordinators are in an important position of leadership, and have a huge impact in preparation for a game? I don't think there's any question about that. I don't think anybody would question that. But I think, ultimately, the responsibility for what happens on the field comes down to me. Because I have the right, when we're planning, to say, "We need to do more of this or more of that," and also have the right to say, "We're doing too much, not enough, not taking advantage of this; is this too complicated for the players?" That's all on me. Now, are we all responsible to some degree? Anybody in a leadership role in the organization is responsible. Everybody has to be accountable for their role. And I've defined those roles. But the ultimate responsibility is with whoever is in charge.

URBAN MEYER: Delegation was very hard for me. Very hard. That was not one of my virtues, delegation. And I generally have a lack of trust that it's going to get done properly, especially when you're dealing with young people and teams. It got to the point at Florida and at Ohio State where you couldn't lose one game. Not one! I would always tell people this isn't the place to put on the training wheels and try to figure it out. But that was not one of my strengths, at all, the delegation of responsibility. I was a micromanager. I got older, and I got a little bit better at it. I tried to learn it. But at times during games things didn't get done the way I wanted them to get done, so that was very hard for me.

KIM MULKEY: Delegation is not difficult for me at all, because I keep continuity in my staff. Now, I've evolved in that area. When I first became the head coach at Baylor University [in 2000], I wanted to do it all, get out of my way, just watch me. But then after about three or four years of doing that, you see that your staff stays with you, they're loyal, they know exactly what you want done and how you want it done. Then, you can delegate. But when you delegate, you better keep them on their toes. My assistants will quickly tell you, in the middle of the night I may send them a text: Did you do this, this and this? Or I may see something I don't like, and I'll ask who was responsible for it. You delegate when you become comfortable with those around you and trust them, and they've been with you a long time.

MACK BROWN: The first thing is hiring. You've got to hire people who fit you and fit your place. When you hire people that fit your philosophy, and they love you and they believe in you, but they're not yes-men, you have a better chance to delegate because they know what you want and expect. And if it gets off track, they're going to come to you and say, "This is what I feel like we want as a program or business." It's not an easy decision. Don't let anybody tell you otherwise. At times I was so hands-on I wouldn't let anybody do anything. And then, at Texas, at the end, I probably allowed too much. I delegated too much, and I allowed people to have opinions— and in some cases change my opinion, when I knew more about it than they did. That is also a mistake. So what I've done is, I've come back and been very, very strong with my opinions, and each position coach is in charge of his room and in charge of his recruits. But they're responsible to me and nobody else. Each coordinator, same thing. I've delegated the responsibility of our team success offensively or defensively to them. They need to have the answers when I ask. It's a big responsibility.

CHRISTIAN HORNER: I've always thought that you don't recruit specialists to do a job, and then tell them how to do it. Part of being a good leader is by identifying talent, and empowering that talent. Especially in an organization of our size, 1,500 people, you can't micromanage everything. You're not efficient, you're not effective if you do [micromanage]. So you need a good leadership team around you that you must empower and trust. With responsibility comes accountability.

NANCY LIEBERMAN: Delegation goes back to trust. You have to trust and empower others to expand your vision. The focus of the CEO and the head coach should be developing a championship organizational strategy. But we also have to let the people we've empowered be key contributors in creating the focus and the strategy that helps fuel success. Employees are people. They're not frickin' assets. And you have to let people know they're valued. It goes back to simple strategies of life. Just make people feel important. We all want to be valued.

JIMBO FISHER: As a head coach and the leader of the organization, there are times when things go wrong when you've delegated to other people. When you coach a guy, and you stand in front of the media, you're responsible for what he does. So, however your players play, that is your responsibility. Sometimes they make mistakes, and you're accountable for everything your players do. Welcome to the head coaching profession.

JOHN CALIPARI: The first thing is, always hire people who are strong in areas that you're weak. That way, everyone around you has a strength that maybe you're not strong at. You talk about guys who have great connections with players. It's hard as a head coach to have the same connection with players that you have when you're an assistant. That's really tough. Assistants can teach you a lot you don't know.

ROY WILLIAMS: That's a great question in the overall scope of leadership. Delegation of responsibility to your staff is something that is earned. It is something that suggests you trust them, and they prove it. I tell them they're my eyes and my ears. They have to have both open to see and hear things I may not see. They have to have both open to make sure that we are truly listening to our players all the time. And I trust them. Whether it's recruiting or things we say or do out on the court.

JIMBO FISHER: We spend a lot of time in our meeting room as an offense, and even with our defensive coaches, because I watch them coach the defense, and how they watch a guy and understand his personality and how he thinks, and who a kid really is. And then we can have a common goal of how we coach him and how we get to him. And making sure you, as the leader, don't get too far away from that. But you've *got* to have delegation. And that's where trusting your coaches comes in, and having them around a lot, and making sure every little thing is done the way you believe it should be done. They need to be extensions of you. It sounds simple. It's not.

TOM IZZO: That's why you better empower some of your assistants and all be on the same page. It goes back to the power of trust we discussed. It's all intertwined.

FRANK BEAMER: We put responsibility on paper. And we started over every year. When we came back from vacation every fall, we got everybody in a room—and I mean everybody. The strength and conditioning staff, the secretaries, the academic people, every single person involved in the organization. And we had a master list. I had a booklet made up, and inside that booklet was everyone's responsibility in the organization. So not only did they know what their responsibility was, but everyone else knew what they were responsible for, too, so you didn't get overlap. As the leader it's important to clearly establish who is responsible for what. I never wanted to be in a position to ask, "Why didn't this get done?" And they answer, "Well, that wasn't my responsibility. Such-and-such should have done that." So I made it crystal clear whose responsibility it was, and who to seek out if something went wrong. And there's another aspect of delegation that I found was important, going back to communication for just a second. As I progressed along, my wife, Cheryl, asked me: "Do you tell your coaches when they do a good job?" And I said, "No, if I don't tell them they're *not* doing a good job, then they know they *are* doing a good job." She said, "Wait a minute, now, don't you like to hear you did a good job? Don't you like to get congratulated?" I said, "Well, yeah, I do. I really like that!" And she told me that my coaches were just the same. That really made me think, and eventually change my approach to communicating with my coaches. After that, I always made a point to go to my coaches—and more times than not, I did so in front of their peers or other players—and tell them what a good job they'd done. That's a better way of leading. You made them feel good, and you did what was right. I learned that from my wife. I've learned a lot of things from my wife.

JIMBO FISHER: My father was the first person to delegate responsibility to me. He really did. And I remember how that felt. My father was always about the whys of the game: "Why did you do this?" And I'd respond, "Well, this guy didn't do it." And he would say, "Well, why didn't you get him to do it?" And I'd say, "That's not my responsibility." And he'd say, "Yes it is. It's your job. You have to understand that, or you're not a leader." My dad was a boss in a coal mine. He was a tough, hard guy. And he was demanding. And his group usually had the most coal. If something needed to be done, he got down and dirty and got it done with them. He showed me how leadership affects people the most.

In my coaching career, [College Football Hall of Fame Florida State football coach] Bobby Bowden delegated responsibility to me. Then when I was with Nick Saban, and I was a coordinator in the SEC at a very young age at LSU, we were trying to flip that program around and he believed in me. Nick was very influential on me. He was influential on the offense, but he was a total defensive guy. So, those of us on the offensive staff were by ourselves a lot. He trusted me. And the trust that he put in me, and being able to delegate that to me, and all the responsibility he gave me, definitely gave me confidence and allowed me to grow. I had to grow, or I wouldn't have lasted very long.

TOM IZZO: I've taken a lot of football stuff. *God, I love football!* In football you got your offensive coordinator, your defensive coordinator, your special teams coordinator, and when I look at responsibilities, I tell every coach, I'm going to give you a title. You're my offensive coordinator. You're my defensive coordinator. We don't do that very much in basketball. But what that does is, with that title comes specific responsibility. You're my recruiting coordinator. They all want the title. They all want the money that comes with the title. But a lot of times you don't want the responsibility that comes with the title. The great ones do. I have to sell them on that. Make them earn it. Make them learn it. But we're crazy as leaders if we're not good delegators. But in saying that, one thing I've not done a good job of yet is firing people. Great leaders have to fire people. And you hope it never comes to that, but that's something I question myself on.

ROY WILLIAMS: In 1988, I'd spent a decade with Dean Smith. I'd watched and learned from a master of his trade. He was like a father to me. I wanted to make him proud. I'd watched him recruit and develop some of the greatest college basketball players of all time. And during that ten years,

I built more and more equity with him, and he'd delegate some things to me. My gosh, you can't describe the feeling you get when your hero shows he believes in you by handing you responsibility. That's a unique feeling of accomplishment. But then you have to live up to it and be successful in what they ask you to do. So there's also pressure. When I left North Carolina to take the head coaching job at Kansas, I realized how powerful that was for me. The night before I left, I said to Coach Smith, "Coach, I hope I don't embarrass you." And he almost got mad at me. He said, "Stop it, don't you worry about that." I said, "Coach, they had Larry Brown and just won a national championship. This is your school." At that point, he did get mad at me. "The only advice I'll give you is to be yourself. That's all you have to do. Look at your personnel and make sure that your personnel and your philosophy match. Because you'll have to change, because your personnel changes. Just be yourself." That's easy to say. Not always easy to do. But he was right. He was always right.

JOHN CALIPARI: I want my assistants to take responsibility. I want each of my assistants to give me a brief scouting report of the next game. So, they watch tape, and provide their belief on what the opponent does. And by doing that, I know each of them is put in a position that they can interject themselves in time-outs, because they've done their homework. They've watched the tape and the opponent. The responsibility I've given them is important to the outcome of the game and to our overall success. But it's important that I give responsibility to staff. Your voice as the head coach only goes so far. It's good for your team to hear other voices.

ROY WILLIAMS: People say all the time about me, he's so lucky, he's only been at North Carolina and Kansas. When I was at North Carolina as an assistant, I had two practices every day for eight years. I coached the JV team for eight years. I wouldn't give it up. Because I loved the coaching part and the learning part. It wasn't "Okay, our JV team is going to practice two or three times a week for an hour and a half." If the varsity practiced six days, by God, my JV team went six days. If the varsity practiced two and a half hours, by God my JV team went two and a half hours.

And Coach Smith said, "Just go be yourself. I have no worries. I have no concerns. I have no doubts. You're going to be great." He'd given me responsibility and seen me succeed. And it was one of the most emotional, satisfying moments of my life. I looked at him and said, "Coach, I just want to make you proud." And I sat down in the car and drove off, tears in my eyes. So for me, what he did was gave me a tremendous amount of confidence. He exposed me to everything I needed to know as a coach at practice. He gave me responsibility to be ready to handle that. He gave me the attitude that if I didn't feel comfortable about it, study more, work more, figure it out. That was the greatest thing. Every day he made me better prepared to be a head coach. Because every day he made me think more. And when I told him that, he smiled and said, "That's the best thing there is."

NANCY LIEBERMAN: As a leader and head coach, you have to be a great talent manager. You can't hire people that you're just going to fire. I say this all the time: KYP—Know Your Personnel. Know your personnel and develop them as players and people. Don't set people up for failure, set them up for success. In most cases their success directly correlates to yours.

ROY WILLIAMS: The delegation to players is even more important. I tell them they earn leadership by your play, and by your actions. And I tell them, tell me now, are you into this, all in, any objections? If you don't have any objections, then we're all in. And if we're all in, tell me now. I do the delegation to my players—"How about you take care of the freshman and make sure he understands." Delegate responsibility to the players to keep each other in line. It's not that you have to be a tattletale or a snitch. Just grab them and say, "Hey, we're not doing that crap. Hear me? Understand?" Because then they're an important part of the decision-making. They're not just players. They're invested more. They're leaders.

Smith's Sideline Summary: Delegation

- Communicate expectations and get out of the way. If you can't do that, you either have to look at yourself or at your expectations.
- Delegation suggests to people that they are valued, produces positive morale within an organization, and rewards staff for being original, creative, and energetic.
- Open-minded delegation will ultimately educate the leader.
- Delegate to people who are strong in areas that you are weak.
- Don't hire yes-men.
- The CEO should focus on developing a championship organizational strategy, while empowering others to be key contributors in creating the focus and the strategy that helps fuel success.
- Sometimes delegation goes wrong. The responsibility for that falls on the CEO.
- While delegation empowers others, the final decision always belongs to the CEO.

Chapter 5

CULTURE

"In this ever-changing society, the most powerful and enduring brands are built from the heart. Their foundations are stronger because they are built with the strength of the human spirit, not an ad campaign."

—Howard Schultz, CEO, Starbucks

C ulture is the behavioral expectation for every member of
an organization. It is the standard of performance and
self-accountability that is consistently demanded, developed,
and distributed over time until it is the fabric and thread that
blankets every corner of an organization.

And it starts with the CEO.

Culture is not tangible. But you can feel it when you walk
in a building. Nick Saban is renowned for The Process. If ever
there were a description of culture, it is Saban's Process at the
University of Alabama. It is not for everyone. Saban explained
The Process to me as the emotional and physical development of each individual player to become the most prepared,
most accountable version of himself. And that personal
demand, he says, allows the man beside him the opportunity
to become the most prepared, most accountable version of
himself. And man by man, the evolution toward personal best
becomes a movement toward an unwavering standard of self-
accountability and team excellence.

*I am my best self because you are your best self. Outwork
yesterday. Play to the standard, not the scoreboard. If you play
to the standard, the scoreboard takes care of itself.*

The Process is a fundamental life lesson: The greatest in
any field are almost always willing to be coached and coached
hard. They are willing to accept guidance in the insatiable
drive to improve. They live to learn. The greatest don't just

give directives. They live directives. Show me, don't tell me. The weakest follow the greatest, and they either adapt or they get weeded out.

The greatest leaders in the world demand the culture they've developed, while constantly striving to update that culture with honesty, education, and foresight.

KIRBY SMART: Culture is what your players, those you're leading, believe in. Who are they when I'm not looking? That's the culture of a program, and it's created through the players and what they believe in. And the value in that is that your culture drives the locker room when you're not in there. Some coaches will pass through the locker room from time to time, and that's a good thing. But most of the time, coaches aren't in the locker room. So your culture is seen when you're not. Are guys smoking? Vaping? Bad-mouthing? Talking bad about each other? Do you have cliques within the team? Your culture is ever present in that locker room. So if you have a good culture, it attracts other good people to that culture. It has immense value. Because so much of the time we're not physically present to the players, and that culture is what permeates the organization and drives the function of: Are we a culture that works hard or are we a culture of shortcuts? Are we a culture of softness or are we a culture of toughness? Everybody can say what they want: but in that locker room, when there's no coach standing there, no strength coach, no trainer, you find out immediately what kind of culture you have. When I'm not there, are you accountable? That's your culture.

JOHN CALIPARI: The whole idea in our program is the culture is about achievement. The culture here is about being competitive. The culture here is learning to battle and fight like hell for your space [opportunity]. The culture here is about asserting yourself in a situation with really good players everywhere. The culture here tells you I'm going to have to sacrifice so that everybody eats.

DOC RIVERS: I always talk about culture, and I tell my players, culture happens when we turn our backs. Meaning, when you walk away from a tough conversation, or when you walk out of the locker room, what the people you are leading are saying is when culture happens. When I turn my back, if you're saying the right things, you have good culture. That's so vital. Culture is what happens when everybody's together. When you have the right culture, even when guys are separate or in small groups, your culture is still being protected. A player says, "I don't want to do this," and a teammate says, "Nope, that's not the way we talk." Leadership isn't even physically present, and yet your culture is being built and preserved.

DABO SWINNEY: Culture is the environment that everybody is walking around in every single day. It's the most important thing when it comes to the health of the organization. It is the climate in the building. It's how people respond. It determines whether the message is just heard, or if you feel and see the message everywhere in the organization. There's a difference. Culture is how people treat each other. The culture drives the daily focus and habits in the organization. It drives the decision-making, as far as who comes in the door. Do they fit the culture? Not everybody focuses on culture. I do.

TOM IZZO: If I look back, my best effort was those first couple years with Mateen Cleaves and them. It led to a national championship. But the reason I say it was my best effort is simple: I hadn't developed my culture yet. And if you don't have a culture, you can't impose your will. Once you build a culture, you can impose your will on other people. I imposed my will on Cleaves, and everything changed. My team went from a coach-coached team to a player-coached team. And I think, too, when you're becoming a leader, you enable other people to carry your message with them—and for you. It's very powerful. I told Cleaves when I recruited him—everything at that time in the state of Michigan was about the Fab 5—and I told him, we can do that here, and you can be the leader of that. And when Mateen and I were standing on the floor in Indianapolis at the Final Four [in 2000], and we stood there together watching "One Shining Moment" and saying, "We did it!" That's when everything changed for me. My culture was established right then.

MACK BROWN: Culture goes back to that consistency and trust we talked about. The players have to know everything we do, and why we do it. Every decision I make, I talk to them about it. We talk about race. We talk about politics. We talk about everything we do. That's where we build trust. People don't understand that, and they think I'm too nice and too soft. The truth is, I'm really hard on the coaches and I'm really hard on the players. I'm very direct with them. Our culture comes down to unity, in every way.

DOC RIVERS: Who are you when I'm not watching? We did this thing with the Celtics, ubuntu. Ubuntu is the way of life. The South Africans used it in its infancy to kind of create the culture of Africa. And we used it with the Celtics. We talked in terms, like, a person is a person through other people. "I can't be all I can be unless you're all you can be." "I can never be threatened by your good"—that's a big one. Because the better you are, the better I am. So by the end of the 2007–2008 NBA season our whole team would talk in those terms. One time I had a sandwich on the team plane, and [then–Celtics point guard] Rajon Rondo got on a plane and said, "Coach, you're not being ubuntu—you didn't bring a sandwich for everybody!" It was funny. To this day, [former Celtics guard] Tony Allen will call me and the first thing he'll say is, "Hey Coach, ubuntu." We literally bought into ubuntu and sold it to each other, and it became our mantra. Ubuntu!

LEONARD HAMILTON: The first thing to develop in a great culture: They have to know you care about them and that you have their best interests at heart. And you can't treat everybody the same. One of the most challenging things to do is change a person's personality. I don't think we have to change them. We have to reprogram them to accept the effort, energy, mindset that you have to play at to be competitive. So, we have to find ways to get them to reach that place without abusive, old-school, kickin' cans, screaming and hollering, cussin'. That mindset doesn't work anymore. So I'm more patient now. I'm more understanding. I'm more thorough. But I find ways to motivate and hold people accountable when they don't really know they're being held accountable.

CHRISTIAN HORNER: Culture comes from the top down, from the ownership and the leadership. Again, leadership sets that tempo. The culture at Red Bull is very much a can-do attitude, a bit of a maverick attitude. We don't want to just conform and exist. We want to push the boundaries and dare to be different. We want to challenge ourselves every day. We want to make sure that we go the extra yard. That's a crucial element of our culture. Your culture defines who you are and how you operate. And for us, that's everything.

URBAN MEYER: When I was at Ohio State, our culture was proven the day [in 2014] our Heisman Trophy–candidate quarterback's arm popped out of his shoulder. [Former Big Ten player of the year, OSU quarterback] Braxton Miller...

Oh my gosh...Right then you learn how strong your culture is, and if you can depend on it. Some people around the college football world thought our season was over. We won the national championship that year. That was because we had an established culture and great players. It was a testimony to all the things I've believed in and worked toward, and what I was raised on. And that the three parts of the culture at Ohio State have always been for us: Relentless Effort; Embrace the hard work; Embrace each other and love each other. That's called Power of the Unit. Those three pieces were on full display that season. That's why we won it all. Obviously, it was a very talented team—but we beat the hell out of some very talented teams, too.

DABO SWINNEY: At Clemson, we say Best Is The Standard, which is not about being *the* best. It's about being *your* best. It's about doing *your* best. When you're focused on being the best, you compare yourself to others. That's not what we're trying to do. When you focus on being *your* best or doing *your* best, maybe you can become *the* best. But you ain't ever gonna be *the* best until you learn how to do and be *your* best. So it's very much an inside-out approach.

NICK SABAN: The Alabama Football annual goals pyramid downstairs in the Crimson Tide football center does not say, "Win the SEC Championship." It doesn't say, "Win the National Championship." It says, "Be a Champion." [It displays] the things you have to do to be a champion. And if you can do those things, you have a chance to win a championship. So, if your focus is on the championship, are you really focused on doing the things you need to do to get there?

TOM IZZO: Our culture goes back to when we won the NCAA championship [in 2000]. I saw a bunch of guys that were a little bit undisciplined, not great students, but I got to the point where those kids graduated and we'd won four Big Ten championships in a row. And I saw how those guys bought in and changed my culture at Michigan State University. Built it, even. I had no culture when I started. I didn't know what my culture would be. We built a football team on hardwood. Tough as hell. Physically tough. Mentally tough. Putting time in. Relentless work. Blue-collar mentality. Decades have passed, and that's still exactly who we are.

JOHN CALIPARI: Play to your training. I think I got that philosophy from *Pound the Stone*, or I got it from one of the books I was reading that talked about it. *Chop Wood, Carry Water*, it might have been that book. But there was a book I read that talked about fall-to-your-training, and it just created a clearer picture for me of what we always say: *Do what we do.* That's my comment. We do what we do. Before I get off the bus, I grab my briefcase and say, "Let's do what we do." *Play to your training* created a better picture for me. You don't have to think. Do what we trained you to do.

GREG SANKEY: To me, you have to have the right people, and it actually starts with their outlook. I've said to our staff: I'm not responsible for your happiness. Whether you're challenged by the work, and it provides you fulfilment, that's up to you.

DABO SWINNEY: So we have Best Is The Standard. We also talk about being ALL IN. It's very important that you have a clearly defined common purpose in the organization. To be your best, you've got to be ALL IN. What's that mean? That means you're *committed* to being and doing your best. ALL IN is an acronym: It's **Attitude**, it's **Love**, it's **Learn**, it's **Invest**, and it's **Now**. It's very important that you have a message that resonates with your audience that they can understand in a succinct way. With young people, especially, I think you've got to have a daily focus. It's critical for any leader, whether you're leading a football team or a Fortune 500 company, to have a clearly defined vision that you can articulate the purpose of the organization in a succinct way.

KIRBY SMART: I'm hell to deal with. I'm 24/7 on top of it. Pressing, wanting everything checked, checking all the boxes and making sure that we're filling up the buckets in every facet we can. But you can't do that without a large staff. You can't do that without support. You can't do that without buy-in from the players. So I think our staff and our administration connects with our players. And we sell Georgia-over-self.

And when your team culture buys into that, that's when you get something rare and special.

ROY WILLIAMS: Another key part of culture is that they see the work. All of it. Not just the time on the court. They see the planning, the preparation, the things I say and the things I do. *WE* do. I'm more comfortable saying "we" because it is—and it has to be—an all-in approach for my assistants, too. Our players know—and they have to know—if they need something, we're there for them. Period. No questions asked. If you *want* something, that's totally different than *needing* something. So tell me how important this is, if you want it.

LEONARD HAMILTON: Sensitive, caring, respectful coaches, man, can pretty much go into any field and adjust. Because of the instincts and the caring we learn and cultivate, and the technical skills and repetition, doing things over and over again to develop people within your culture. That applies to just about everything you do in life.

DOC RIVERS: Back to ubuntu for a moment, it is, "I am, because you are." I can't be all I can be, unless you are all you can be. The biggest failure of teams is when success comes and jealousy sets in. When you are no longer threatened by someone else's success, because you realize the more successful your teammate is, the more successful you will be, it is *extremely* powerful.

TOM IZZO: If you have a good culture, hopefully your seniors pass it down. That's what I love about football and hate about basketball—we have this one-and-done stuff now [in basketball], so you don't get to pass down your culture. That puts more pressure on a coach in basketball than even in football. Every single year you have to redevelop it and redefine it. And you do that by spending time with guys, getting guys to trust you. Realizing your title is not going to impose trust. Time, attention, listening, and follow-through earn trust. You can lean on your title and your résumé to say, "I won a national championship, I've gotten guys to the NBA, I've won a lot of games." But that isn't going to solve your problems, in my opinion. And to make sure the culture is passed down, I utilize my former guys. When Magic Johnson comes back—and he comes back a lot—Steve Smith, Mateen Cleaves, I take guys from each era who have been here, I bring them in and they talk about similar things I preach. There are no secrets to being great. There aren't. None. Show them the work that earns their respect. I try to be able to back my opinions up, and sometimes I need help! Because kids don't want to believe the parent! They don't want to believe the coach! So as a leader, I lean on undeniable proof to reach my players. Okay, Magic, come talk to them for me. Reach them for me. Okay, Steve Smith is delivering the message now. He *was them* at a very high level! He was the all-time leading scorer in school history when he left here! All-American! NBA champion! Gold medalist! When it's those guys talking, the players take in the information differently. Using those past success stories as examples for what the guys I'm leading now can become, is one reason I've been able to maintain a distinct, successful culture.

TIM CORBIN: Excellence doesn't necessarily mean winning the national championship. Excellence doesn't mean performing at the highest level, above everyone else, on a daily basis. Excellence is reaching a level internally where you reach a different plateau, you move to a different level, because you start to understand the decisions and choices you make benefit you in what you're doing, and as a result you're benefitting the team. To me, that's the greatest sign of excellence—bettering yourself so you can better the team.

KIM MULKEY: Culture is a lot like the personality of a coach. If you see a coach on the sideline that is passive, most of the time their teams aren't very aggressive. They might be very good, might be very talented. But they're not going to be *aggressive.* You see an energetic, enthused, intense, passionate coach, you're going to see a team that flat gets after it. I firmly believe that: The product on the floor is a reflection of the coach on the sideline.

DABO SWINNEY: Building a culture is a daily task. Everybody has their different path as to how they do it. For us at Clemson, we do it through family atmosphere, we do it through relationships, we're very much a relationship-driven place and a purpose-driven place. We instill our core values daily, simple things like respect. Communication is vital to a good culture. You have to have accountability. You have to have a culture that develops leadership, that leads to trust and respect, a genuine appreciation for each other. Ultimately, a good culture comes down to the people that you choose to be a part of the journey with you.

URBAN MEYER: The leader leads the culture. And effort was always the focus of our culture. We want our players to play without fear of making a mistake. We believe "effort" will overcome mistakes. Effort is measurable, and there are sound bites used to evaluate effort: 4-to-6, A-to-B, + 2.

- 4-to-6: Four to six seconds is the average length of a play. Go as hard as you can for four to six seconds.
- A-to-B: every play has a starting point (A) and a finish point (B). Go as hard as you can from A to B.
- + 2: + 2 is a mentality/expectation. It's the finish. When we ask you to do ten reps, do twelve. Always take two steps past the whistle. The finish is the most important part of any situation.

DOC RIVERS: You have to create standards. I have a thing that I tell my staff, and it's very simple: It's called "You Go First." We say about players, they gotta do this or that. Well, how about you go do it first! We say, "Our players need to learn how to be a good teammate." Well, you go first! I say it all the time to my coaches. We'll say, "One of our players needs to work harder!" You do it first! You show it first! If you show it first, they will follow!

KIRBY SMART: I think you have to confront and demand, and some people don't want to do that nowadays. They're like "You know what, I'm just going to let that slide and let that guy do what he wants." Well, there's a certain way I think it has to be done. And if you don't do it that way, then I tend to disagree with it, and I want to confront demand and make sure it's done the right way. There's certain non-negotiables when you get into this organization.

URBAN MEYER: When Braxton Miller got hurt, it was seven or eight days before our first game [of 2014] against Navy. Our backup quarterbacks didn't have one single competitive rep between them. Not one. [Their names were] J. T. Barrett and Cardale Jones. Many of us were not confident that they had the ability to play. And here we have the back-to-back Big Ten Player of the Year, Heisman Trophy candidate, made the decision to come back to school for his senior year, and seven days before the first game, his labrum pops for the second time. He curls up in a ball on the ground. I remember holding his hand. He was crying and I was crying with him. Lay on the ground with him. Held his hand. Then reality sets in. That reality is: Game on. How strong is your culture? How strong are you and your staff as leaders? Because you are in it now. Adversity is when leadership and culture get challenged. That was one of the most adverse situations I ever faced. Throughout the course of the year, we didn't realize it until it was done, but our staff and the culture of the program were as good as I've ever been around. That's the only way it worked.

NICK SABAN: Mediocre people don't like high achievers. And high achievers don't like mediocre people. So if everybody doesn't buy into the same principles and values of the organization, at the same high standard, you're never going to be successful. That is a big part of our culture [at Alabama].

GREG SANKEY: We set an expectation in the SEC office that you never complain down the org chart, or on an equal level on the org chart. Always complain up. In my experience, you can sit around with colleagues and complain, but nobody ever does anything about it other than just complain. So if there's a real issue, rather than just murmuring among each other, elevate it, because maybe there's an answer that would make you take a step back and say, *Oh, okay, I get it.* Or maybe you'll bring about change. And at the end of the day, just talking at that colleague level doesn't help resolve anything.

JOHN CALIPARI: We teach servant leadership. That's an important aspect of our culture. I think about when [the 2010] Haiti [earthquake] hit, and with the devastation of that island, we did a telethon. When Superstorm Sandy hit [in 2012], that group did a telethon. In both cases, we raised more than $1 million. I believe we did one for Houston [Hurricane

Harvey, in 2017], and I brought the twins [Aaron and Andrew Harrison] back with me, and maybe Jarred Vanderbilt came with me, too. We went back to see where the money that we had raised was going. And you want them to know, and to see, that you can use the leverage you have to help others. That's basic servant leadership. And Michael Kidd-Gilchrist was the one that, we were playing in the championship game of the SEC and had won 20-some games in a row, and he came in prior to the game and said, "Let Darius [Miller] start in my place." I said, "What are you talking about? Are you sick?" He said, "No, but we need him to play well for us to win a national title, and he's not playing well." The year before, he was the MVP of the tournament. Michael knew he had played well the previous year. This year, in two games, he hadn't scored one basket. So I start him. Michael struggles. It's the only game he didn't start all year, and we end up losing at the end of the game to Vanderbilt. But because of that servant leadership he displayed—caring more about the other than yourself—we win the national title. I would say that's the glaring example of when servant leadership helped our program. And Michael was the youngest freshman in the country, so when someone tells you you've got to be older to make those decisions, that's not true. I don't want to take all the credit, but the way we do things at Kentucky, plus his mother and father and how he was raised, played big roles. That stands out for me. The communication made its way to the player, and the culture was evident.

DOC RIVERS: I learned very early on that we as leaders have to show them, not just tell them. My first job coaching, my very first meeting, we were talking about the players on the team. And one of the coaches said, "This guy, he's a headache. He's always late, always talking." And I said, "Has anyone told him?" And they said, "Well, if you tell him, he'll get mad." And I'm laughing. I'm like "So you're mad at something a player is doing, and yet, he doesn't know he's doing it because no one told him? That's insane!" So I said, "How about we go first? How about we show the way, us being the example." And when you do that as a leader, the players want to follow you. And players want to be coached. This new thing that players don't want to be coached is a bunch of crap. They want to be coached—but they want to be coached for purpose. To achieve something, and you have to show them the right way.

JOHN CALIPARI: I tell my guys when we go to a hotel, "The reason you treat everybody with respect, the people cleaning your room, the people serving your meals, the people at the front desk, those were our mothers and fathers. All of us here! And would you disrespect your mother or father? Or would you want someone else to do it, because of the position they have as hardworking people? You treat them with respect!" It's part of those pillars of this program that a small act of kindness can have an unbelievable impact, because you're in this [University of Kentucky] uniform, because you're able to do good will in the community. Trying to get them to understand. You sign autographs, you take pictures, you make time, you ask questions. When someone comes up to you ask them, "Where are you from? Why are you here? What is it?" And let them tell you their story. That's all part of being a leader at Kentucky, that when they leave us, I tell them, "You're going to have fame and fortune. Fame is fleeting and money has wings. This is about the impact you have while you're in the seat you're in." And I say the same thing about coaching at Kentucky: If you sit in the office and all you do is watch tape, you're cheating the position. You have a chance to impact people. You have an obligation to impact people.

MACK BROWN: Common purpose is another thing I got from General Odierno. I asked him, "You've got all these kids over here [in war] that are average age nineteen years old, they're sitting here with two or three kids at home—and they reenlist? What's that about?" He said, "It's common purpose. We all buy into a common purpose. And that common purpose is taking care of the man on your right, taking care of the man on your left. That common purpose is keeping America safe. And these guys and ladies have a better and more respected and more powerful position over here [in war] than they do in America." So we build everything in our football family, and we talk about it all the time: Communication. Trust and respect. Common purpose. Our common purpose being: We want to have fun; we want to graduate. We want to prepare our life for life after football. And lastly, we want to win all the games. Those are the four principles. That is our common purpose and those are the principles that we base *everything* off of. The vulnerability for us is we're constantly looking for better ways to do things. We tell our guys, "We'll steal ideas. We're constantly looking for ways to do those four things better. We want you to have fun. But we have to win. But you have to graduate. And we're doing all this because we're helping prepare you for life after football."

URBAN MEYER: Parts of our culture are nonnegotiable. Number one is **Relentless Effort**. Be fearless. Don't worry about making mistakes. A team that plays fast is because they're confident and fearless, not worried about making mistakes. Number two is **Competitive Excellence**. That means we're going to work harder than everyone else. Embrace it and don't bitch about it. Be ready mentally and physically to make the play when your number is called. And the last one, the most powerful form of inspiration, is love and ownership. We call that **Power of the Unit**.

JOHN CALIPARI: If you're drinkin', smokin', carpet-chasin', you shouldn't come here [to my team]. Because that does not work here. If you want to be promised you'll start, or [get a number of] shots or minutes or all that, you shouldn't come here. You earn that here. If you're better than all the guys we have, you're going to start. If they're better than you, they're going to start. Simple.

MACK BROWN: Two things are very important to me in my life in coaching, and they're directly responsible for our culture: (1) I want to be fair. And I want to be fair to everybody I deal with. And (2) I want to be consistent. I had a recruit's dad tell me once, "Coach, you need to give me something for my son." I said, "What's that?" He said, "I need you to give me the gift of consistency." I said, "Okay, tell me what that means." He said, "My son likes you today. I want him to like you tomorrow. I want him to like you in three years and in ten years. That's really important to me, that this is not a recruiting pitch, but that this is who you really are." And I said, "Got it. That's all fair." So that's who we are. That's our culture.

JIMBO FISHER: People get bored with details. I think we get away from the details and take things for granted. I always say, "Don't get bored." You'll hear me say that a thousand times to our players. "Don't. Get. Bored. Come with the same intensity every day. Come with the same attention to detail every day." That's our culture. Because those are learned behaviors. Those are habits. People say, "We have bad habits." Well, why do you have bad habits? Because you got bored doing things the right way. Boredom is something we don't talk about a lot, taking it for granted. I'm bored by doing that same thing over and over and over again, the right way. I take it for granted, and gradually the fine details of it slip, and all of a sudden an inch becomes two inches, two inches becomes four, four becomes eight, and all of a sudden you got a foot, and then two feet, and it's too far to ever bring back. Don't. Get. Bored. And don't let boredom enter your culture. If you do, you're screwed.

NICK SABAN: I don't think it's fair to create the expectations for the team before they ever have a body of work. But that's the nature of the beast in this day and age. I think being able to handle that—not putting pressure on yourself to try to live up to that expectation—creates a lot of anxiety. You put pressure on yourself, which means you're focused on outcome, not process. When I say you've got to focus on what it takes to win, and enjoy winning, that's what I'm talking about—not the pressure to win, and then the *relief when you win*, rather than the *joy that you won*. There's a difference in all that. You've got to be able to handle that, and not let it affect you.

TOM IZZO: There has to be a point for everybody when culture changes. Mike Krzyzewski talks about his 1986 team, how they all bought in after he'd almost been fired. Everybody has that point of demarcation that sets a new standard for good. "For good" used to be "forever." But now it's ever changing. Because I can't keep guys sometimes more than one or two years. Guys either transfer or go pro. We can't just sit back and say, Bobby Bowden's culture takes over. Bobby Knight's culture takes over. These guys that did for all those years. Even Krzyzewski had to look at it and say, "Is this one-and-done thing the right way to go? I haven't won a conference championship in like ten years." We do have to adjust to the times. But adjustment doesn't mean you're giving in. It means you're making sure you're listening and watching, rather than talking.

GREG SANKEY: You want to set an expectation. So we use the phrase: The SEC Expectation of Excellence. Now, I've never defined it. I've probably given examples. What I've said is, "Our teams are expected to win national championships, so how do *we* perform at that level?" That's the expectation of excellence for the Southeastern Conference.

URBAN MEYER: At Ohio State, every Wednesday for us in the spring, we do training on people for how they get careers, from physical responsibility to how to interview. Every person, by their junior year, has to have a working résumé. We have people come in and talk to them about the interview process, about what to wear. We buy them a suit, buy them an iPad, send them out to shadow people every year to be really focused on what they want to do. Eighty to 85 percent of Americans hate their jobs because they don't research it. They don't look around. And then they get stuck. Our job as educators is to get them out there. So you're mandated at Ohio State to go out and shadow opportunities first and second year, and third year we get you an internship. And fourth year we get you a job. That all started because of my daughter. My daughter's recruitment changed everything. It was the advent of Real Life Wednesdays. For many years, the whole expectation of college sports was the degree. And when I went on recruiting trips with my daughter, I sat on the parents' side. All they're talking about is locker rooms and training tables. Why are we talking about this? I want to know what you're going to do for my kid. The answer that always came back was, "We're going to help her get a degree." She's a 4.0. I don't want to devalue a degree, but a lot of people have degrees. And student athletes, the way we handled our business, like a lot of schools, was, get the kid in school, make sure they graduate, and you move them on. To me, that's using people. I guess when it's someone else's kid I never really thought of it. But when it came to being my kid it changed everything. No longer was a degree the final stage. That degree was an expectation. That was an evolution for preparing people for life after sport.

JOHN CALIPARI: The point of it is, guys may not be happy with their position, but no one was promised things that we could not deliver on and come through on. I may look at a guy and say, "Could you even play thirty minutes a game? Like, if we need you to play thirty minutes, could you play for thirty minutes?" I only say that to say, you're good enough to do it— but I can't do it for you. I don't have a magic wand. I can't compete for you. I'm not on the court for you. You've got to do it. That goes back to culture.

TOM IZZO: One reason I've had success: I have talent on my teams, but I don't have boatload of McDonald's All Americans here. And yet every three years we're in the Final Four. That's because I convince guys that, if you're not really good, then this is why you should be, you can win championships and play in the NBA. I talk about the NBA constantly. A lot of coaches avoid that. The old adage, "If you don't dream it, you'll never achieve it." I believe that. I think you should discuss it. Don't be obsessed with it. But it should be in your culture.

JOHN CALIPARI: The relationships you have along the way mean more and more as you get older. And it's not just blowing through life. I have a thread with my high school teammates on it. I have a thread with my college teammates on it—from Wilmington and from Clarion. You have friends you make and relationships you create that are as important as anything you're doing on that journey. I've just been fortunate enough to be around so many good people that I had a chance to do what I did. I always say: There are so many coaches who are better than I was, but I had opportunities they didn't have. I worked hard. They worked hard, too. And I always say, fate intervened, sometimes good, sometimes bad, sometimes earned, sometimes not earned. Fate intervened in a very big way for me. So all I tried to do was stay the course—if you make it about the kids, make it about everybody else, it seems to go good for you. Those relationships become part of your culture, too.

LEONARD HAMILTON: Bobby Bowden was extremely religious, so he made it easy on the rest of us! He had a prayer meeting after every touchdown, right there on the sideline! I loved it! But from a moral standpoint, I have to be careful not to impose my faith on my players, because it might be offensive to some people. So you handle that in a respectful way, but it's important because it helps you with your moral compass. As a coach, it's part of my culture. You've got to create that atmosphere of doing what's right, but we're going to work hard and do it the right way. And that's where you have success. We've had probably nineteen kids drafted in twenty years. That means our system works. So now, you've got kids buying into a way because they can see what can happen if they buy in.

JOHN CALIPARI: Arrogance is the great evil. You forget the path and you become arrogant, like success is just supposed to happen. Especially at a place like Kentucky. You put on a Kentucky uniform, you think you're supposed to win. What we continue to try to get kids to do is fall back on the training. If we can get them to prepare at a high level in practice every day, they fall back on that training when it matters, when they need it. And if you're not doing that daily, what ends up happening is they end up leaning where they choose to go, which is what's easy.

NICK SABAN: The greatest threat to excellence or sustained success is complacency—the blatant disregard for doing what's right. So I think you try to keep the players focused on the process, and how they can create value for themselves and their future by how they perform and how they play. I think that's the most important thing that they'll relate to—because it affects them directly. It's still difficult to still have the team concept—everybody bought into the principles and values of the team doing the right thing. But if you have good leadership on your team, that impacts it as much as anything.

Smith's Sideline Summary: Culture

- Culture is what those you're leading in an organization believe in.
- The leader leads the culture.
- Good culture requires consistent adjustments and upgrades. Adjusting culture doesn't mean changing the culture, but keeping it current and relevant.
- Culture happens when backs are turned. Who are we when leadership isn't looking?
- Great culture happens when those you're leading know you care about them.
- Never be threatened by someone else's good. Because the better you are, the better I am. I am because you are. Ubuntu!
- Complaining down the org chart is a waste of time. For answers or change, complain up.
- Servant leadership is powerful. Show me, don't tell me.
- Fame is fleeting and money has wings.
- Mediocre people don't like high achievers. And high achievers don't like mediocre people.

Chapter 6

CRISIS MANAGEMENT

"When written in Chinese, the word crisis *is composed of two characters. One represents danger and the other represents opportunity."*

—John F. Kennedy, 35th President of the United States.

Inevitably at some point a leader must face a crisis. It may be failure to produce as expected, individually or collectively. It may be family tragedy or personal issues. It may be violations of human resources code within the business. It may be low morale or disinterest. The definitions are innumerable, and contexts only compound the potential for crises. What may seem insignificant initially could prove to be quite detrimental if allowed to fester. It may be a singular event, a shocking development, or chronic mismanagement. But eventually, it must be addressed by leadership.

In mid-February 2023 there was a horrific mass shooting at Michigan State University, which claimed the lives of three MSU students and critically injured five others. The tragedy rocked the school, the state, the nation. In the days that followed, as the Spartans' basketball program prepared to play bitter cross-state rival Michigan amid trying to rationalize the irrational, head coach Tom Izzo struggled to coach his team. Izzo awoke on game day, February 18, unable to locate words he believed could properly galvanize his men in the wake of tragedy. What could he say that might possibly offer perspective when basketball seemed so trivial?

He turned on the television.

I was on the screen.

I was in Raleigh, North Carolina, that morning, standing on ice, wearing ice skates, outfitted nose to toes in bulky, restrictive hockey goalie padding. It smelled like a four-passenger car carrying five teenage boys and a Taco Bell Party Pack. Gracious, it stunk. The stank lingered. I'm not sure you could exorcise that stank with Ajax and a blowtorch.

I'd ice-skated just once in my life, never played hockey, and certainly never stood in goal with four college hockey players gleefully firing slapshots at my face. I could barely see out of the helmet. The bars shielded my eyes from clarity. The chest and leg padding was fitted for a six-foot-four, 220-pound, twenty-year old college male. I am six feet, 165, and pushing forty-seven years old at this time. Mobility is limited. Flexibility barely existent, especially at seven forty-five in the morning before all my creaky ol' ball joints were lubed. My waist size is thirty. The girdle I was wearing, which in its pouch held the protective hard plastic cup in place, had a waistband that looked to be approximately size thirty-six. I was concerned for my man region. I had substantial fear the cup would slip out of position just as a puck hit me in the junk. There was a lot going on.

So as the North Carolina State University Hockey Team, the Ice Pack, hit shot after shot in my direction, and I progressively looked more and more awkward, the comedy of errors escalated.

This was all happening on live television—ESPN's signature show, *SportsCenter.*

In my position, you hope it's both entertaining and educational. That *E* in ESPN? It stands for *Entertainment.* Serving sports fans anytime, anywhere, is our ethos. Entertainment is the first tenet in that passion.

I've never been scared to take chances or risk injury in the name of entertainment. I've done some wild shit, too: a back-flip into a pool from a ten-meter concrete high dive at the University of Miami that angered Lainie worse than nearly any other shenanigans I've pulled in more than twenty years of marriage. I've strapped up with tethers and grabbed the trapeze bar at Florida State (FSU has circus school!). I've ridden a Vespa around a chaotic traffic circle in Rome, wearing a large, white, open-faced motorcycle helmet with red and green stripes that gave me a striking resemblance to Luigi in Mario Kart. I once dressed out in full Alabama Crimson Tide uniform and pads to run the forty in Tuscaloosa. I've caught punts at Tennessee. Hell, I've even wrestled steers in Texas. But this goalie moment was different. I didn't sense the same ability to control the situation I typically feel.

I did it anyway. I have infinite trust in my field producer and brother, Patrick Abrahams. To steal Kirby Smart's analogy from the "Communication + Listening" chapter, if Patrick writes it and I sing it, it always works. The players toyed with me. I barely got a glove on a single puck. I managed to shuffle my body into the flight path a couple times, and a puck happened to hit my chest or the padding protecting my leg. I laughed with the anchors. I tried to deliver witty quips while audibly sucking wind. Regardless of how awkward or foolish I looked, I was all in. For me, the joy in the job is the shared experience and real-time energy exchange—those of us within our team who collaborate to create, and those of you at home enjoying your Saturday morning coffee with a laugh.

It wasn't until later that day that I learned a deeper scope of that moment.

Midway through my weekly SEC Network program, *Marty & McGee*, my phone buzzed.

It was Izzo.

In a lengthy text message, Coach explained to me that that afternoon his Spartans would suit up for their first game since the campus shooting tragedy. They would play hated rival Michigan. He'd been struggling mightily to reach his team. He wasn't sure how to find the delicate balance between the self-described "Izzo prick" who confronts, demands, and follows through in the quest to push his young men beyond what they believe is possible, and the father figure who always has the proper words, tone, and compassion. He said watching me flail about attempting to play goalie was a reminder of the platform with which he'd been blessed. So many people in East Lansing and beyond were mourning unspeakable loss. And the Spartans, on that day, could offer those people a two-hour escape from horror.

"This morning you gave me a five-minute escape," Izzo wrote. "Thank you, my brother. You did what great people do. You stepped outside the box and made a little fun of yourself. In a very tough day, I escaped for a moment. And I want to thank you for that. So from a thousand miles away, I want you to know you've helped a basketball coach deal with something Jud [Heathcote, legendary Michigan State coach and Izzo's mentor] didn't teach me. You can't teach how to deal with this. Seriously, thank you for giving me a chance to escape. THAT will be my rallying cry tonight!

"PS: Watching you play goalie, I think I'd keep my day job if I were you."

When I read Izzo's note during a *Marty & McGee* commercial break, I cried.

I couldn't believe what I was reading. Izzo reminded me that vulnerability is so powerful. We never know what someone else is managing emotionally. And we never know what light we might offer them when they're cloaked in darkness. In crises as a leader, there is often no guide or playbook to reference for answers. But as the leader, you're the one who's supposed to have the answers everyone else seeks. The stories you're about to read intricately detail moments of sorrow, pain, and uncertainty, and how some of the best leaders in the history of sport managed them.

MACK BROWN: When one of my players at Texas died in a truck crash, Cole Pittman, they called me and said, "Coach, we have a young man that we can't identify. There's no identification. But he's got a Cotton Bowl ring, and the Cotton Bowl ring's got Cole Pittman's name on it. And we would like for you to send us a picture and confirm that that's him." I did. It was him. And then they said, "We'd like for you to call the parents and inform them that they've lost their son. But at the same time, you need to make sure that they have a high school coach there, a principal there, and don't say he died. Because they could try to commit suicide, or they could try to harm themselves, or go into shock and have heart attacks. This is a real critical time." So I did all that. And I'll never forget, the dad said, "I want you to come and speak at the funeral." And I said, "Dad, I can't. I can't do that. There's no way I could do that." And the dad said, "I'm gonna be speaking at the funeral, and I'm the father. So you can do this, too. You've got to do it." And I did that. I don't even remember what I said. But it's on video. I've got it. I've never looked at it. Then, about a week later [pauses extensively to collect his thoughts], we had a memorial—six hundred athletes at Texas—for Cole. And I was supposed to go and explain to those six hundred athletes why this was okay. And about death. And about losing a friend. All that. And I did that. I got up that morning, and I said to [my wife] Sally, "What an awful day to be the head football coach at Texas, because I've got to go talk to these kids about something that confuses even me, so I'm not even sure what I should be doing or saying." And she said, "No. You're looking at this the wrong way. What a wonderful day for you to be the head football coach at the University of Texas, because this gives you the opportunity to explain this to these kids, and that's your job. Your job is to make this okay." And she was right. And I was wrong. So I went, I did a great job, handled it, and she was right, it was my job. The first thing we discussed in this conversation was leadership, and leadership is taking crises and turning them into positives. And that's what I had to do on that day. It wasn't easy. Far from it. But it was necessary.

TOM IZZO: My star player's brother committed suicide two days before we started the 2019–2020 season. That was a crisis for which there's no book. Jud Heathcote didn't leave me with that knowledge. I can't call Nick Saban or Steve Mariucci on that. All I could do was learn as I went. It was one of the most difficult things I've ever had to do as a leader, because there's no road map. I called [NFL Hall of Fame and Super Bowl-winning coach] Tony Dungy, and talked to different psychiatrists and grievance counselors, and got as much insight as I could. That's another thing some leaders do: When they get into key leadership positions they're done learning. They believe, *I've mastered my craft. I got it now.* Not me. I'm still learning at sixtysomething.

ROY WILLIAMS: In crises as a leader, you've got to be calmer than they are. You've got to be reassuring. They've got to trust you.

DOC RIVERS: A big crisis for me was when I was the head coach of the Los Angeles Clippers, and the owner, Donald Sterling, said a bunch of racist things. And I had to walk into a room full of players, who were upset, and they wanted to be upset at anybody connected to the owner. And I was the coach. I was the general manager. And I'm working for this owner who had said a bunch of racist things. People don't realize the detail that you have to have as the leader. I remember before I walked into that meeting with these angry players, I had to decide, *Do I wear my Clippers shirt, or don't I?* That's how much detail I had to consider. So I decided, *I'm the coach of this team, and I have to keep this team afloat. So I'm gonna wear my Clippers shirt, because we're about to have practice.* And when I walked in, I was the only one wearing a Clippers shirt. The players didn't have the [Clippers] shirt on. Only I had it on. And I realized, *This may not be the right decision.* And I started talking to my players, and I realized within thirty seconds that they were not listening. They were angry. They were mad—I even felt like they were mad at me! And I had some notes that I had written to talk to them about the situation, and I put the notes down on the table in front of them, so they could see me turn it over. And I turned to them, and I said, "I want you to know, my name is Glenn Rivers. Not Doc Rivers. I grew up in a suburb of Chicago that was very rough. My dad was a cop. My mom worked on an assembly line. And I'm a Black man. And there's no one in this room who has seen more racism than me. And there is no one in this room who is more upset at Donald Sterling than me." And when I finished those thoughts, everyone sat up. They remembered who I was, instead of who they saw me as for a moment. I had to remind them that I am them. And then

I had to lead them through a crisis that could have gone really, really bad, in my opinion.

KIRBY SMART: I've never had a hurdle greater as a leader than when we lost Devin Willock and Chandler LeCroy in a tragic car accident, right after we won the national championship in 2023. I don't know that I ever will have a greater hurdle. I hope not. Losing a young staff member, in Chandler, who shined such a bright light on this entire organization, with a positive attitude all the time. And Devin was an incredible player, who was incredibly kind and a great leader. That was the largest crisis management moment I've had, the loss of life of these two young people. I've coached for more than twenty years, and I'd never lost a player. For that to happen, and to face all of our players in the midst of that and have to call and explain to parents that they've lost a child, there is no way to describe how difficult that is. There is no defined way to deal with it. So when you write the book on crisis management, you can throw it away. Because nobody can tell you how to grieve. Nobody can tell you how to manage a situation like that, other than through your own feelings and emotions. We had kids who wanted to talk about it and kids who didn't want to talk about it. We had kids who wanted to cry and kids who didn't want to cry. We had kids who had just gotten here and didn't know Devin or Chandler, and they didn't even know how to act. And none of that is wrong. It's a crisis that you only get through together. It probably brings you tighter, closer-knit, because you're reminded to appreciate one another on a human level more. You hug each other more. You say *I love you* more often. That's the biggest thing I've learned—we probably don't do those things enough as football coaches.

FRANK BEAMER: On April 16, 2007, was the worst crisis you could imagine. That was the day of the campus shooting at Virginia Tech. It was one of the most difficult experiences of my life. Thirty-two people died that day. In the aftermath of that—I'll never forget this, ever, as long as I live—the university wanted me to go over to the hotel on campus. And they had all the families in this room and they wanted me to speak to the families. I went in the room through a side door and turned to the front of the room. And I got to a podium, and when I turned around, I'll never forget the eyes of all those moms and dads and families, and people who had just lost a loved one. To this day, those eyes stay with me. There are no words that help those people at a moment like that. It's just pain and hurt. But I told them that day, "You can count on me. I am here. If you ever need to talk, give me a call. I am praying for you." And through that whole thing, we made the decision that we were not going to let one sick individual define who and what Virginia Tech is. We know who we are. We know how deeply we care about each other. We know how much we got each other's backs. We know how much we share together and what that unity means to us. So one sick individual, even though that's what everyone is talking about, we're going to show the world that's not what or who Virginia Tech is.

URBAN MEYER: Braxton Miller is like my son. I love that kid. Without Braxton Miller we don't win the national championship in 2014. He set the table in 2012. That year we weren't very good. But *he* was very good. And he was unselfish. So when he injured his shoulder in camp [in 2014], I see him curled up in a ball, crying, and my first reaction was to grab his hand and cry right there with him, put my arm around him, and tell him I love him, and we're going to take care of him. Then reality set in. You got [inexperienced backup quarterbacks] J. T. Barrett and Cardale Jones. I can't remember what I said to J.T., but I remember it took him a minute to get going. We lost to Virginia Tech in Game 2. But then J.T. caught fire. And then that other guy came in there, Cardale, and wow. I'll never forget that. That was a time warp. That was the most illogical National Championship ever. Zeke [Ezekiel Elliott] became Zeke. [Joey] Bosa became Bosa. Before J.T. got hurt [against Michigan in the 2014 regular season finale], Zeke was performing okay. But they were different players after that. It was a lot to manage that crisis. But our organization was different after that. Better. Forever.

NANCY LIEBERMAN: Being a female in sports there's always a crisis. We're just getting to levels as head coaches, as CEOs of companies. A very important player for me was struggling with his family. And I thought it was very important to be attentive to what he was going through. And just making sure that he knew that I was accessible as a valued part of their family. It was important to know his kids' names, his family's names, his wife's name. That's really important. I learned this from Kevin Costner, who is a great friend. We were playing ball at the Final Four, and I was going into Manhattan to watch his movie *For Love of the Game*. And every time Kevin Costner called my house, the first thing he said on the phone, because I was a young married person, he would say, "Hey, Tim, this is Kevin Costner. Just checking in on you to see how you're doing, and T.J. is good. And holler back at me when you guys can. Tell Nancy I say hello." That was enormous! Because it wasn't Kevin Costner calling Tim's wife. It was him calling the whole family. That's just brilliant strategy of disarming any crisis, or insecurities. It's a simple gesture, but has profound impact because people feel included. I learned that from Kevin Costner. There's prehab and there's rehab. If you're rehabbing, you didn't handle the crisis well. If you're prehabbing, you're trying to avoid the injury, avoid the crisis. And I try to live my life in prehab.

NICK SABAN: There are so many things that happen in a game that you have to be able to maintain your individual momentum and execute when your best is needed. When an "oh shit" moment comes up in the game, you've got to be able to play the next play. It's the same thing in life. We all have issues and things that happen in life, some we create, some we don't create, we still have to deal with. But you've got to have the right mindset to be able to sustain the right energy level and regain momentum when those things happen. We talk all the time about playing one play at a time for sixty minutes in a game like every play has a history and a life of its own. And no matter what happened on the last play, focus on the next play—don't look at the scoreboard, don't worry about the outcome, just do the things you need to do to get the outcome that you want. Even if you practice well, if you don't go into the game with the right psychological disposition to sustain momentum and how you play, play in and play out, even when things go bad, even when you're playing on the road, it doesn't matter where you're playing, then you're not going to be able to maintain the kind of focus you need to be able to execute.

CHRISTIAN HORNER: You can't have the answers for everything. But you've got to make decisions based on the information that you have. You make as informed a decision as you can. The worst thing you can do is not make any decision. You're not going to get every decision right, but when you make a wrong decision it's recognizing it, not trying to just enforce it, and changing it. You just hope you make more right decisions than wrong decisions.

JIMBO FISHER: Crisis management is part of leadership. And it's instinct. The first thing is recognizing it, and knowing things are going sideways and you have to have a plan. It's like a boat going down. I'm either plugging this hole or we're gonna sink. I think you have to be willing to be open-minded, but also willing to do things out of the box if doing things out of the box is required. You really can never be prepared for a crisis, because you don't know what the crisis is going to be. But you have to have rules and be willing to put yourself out there and communicate, whether it's hard, tough love, holding on to them, whatever is necessary. Those things are instinctive. Sometimes you've got to crank it up and get on everybody. Sometimes you have to just say, "Hey, just calm down, everything is all right." Slow it down. Go back to fundamentals.

JOE GIBBS: In NASCAR there are constant crises. Because you have people, money, occupations, and competition. And when you put those things together, there's going to be dynamics all the time that cause issues. Dealing with that is the leader's world. That's what the leader does. You have to be smart. You don't panic. You listen. You figure out what the problem is, and then you go to work with your trusted team on how to solve it. It's the same thing in football. It's professional sports. It's the best people in the world doing something highly competitive, and money is involved and careers are involved.

NICK SABAN: Sometimes you need a thunderbolt somewhere along the line to get you straightened out, something that happens that gets everybody's attention.

JOHN CALIPARI: The only thing that brings about change in an organization is a crisis. The bigger the crisis, the bigger changes you can make. Having meetings, kumbaya sessions, does not bring about change. A crisis does.

GREG SANKEY: In the COVID experience, there was so much information coming in at any one time that you had your normal full-time job, then 50 percent more trying just to manage COVID. It took over. That experience touched so many areas of leadership for me: crisis management, communication, delegation. Because COVID just *took over*. So you went from managing it, to trying to triage an unimaginable situation. And the first question I was asked was "How are you going to get back to [competition]?" And we had to focus on "How do we get back to anything?" I spent probably three or four weeks trying to touch every conversation group. We appointed a medical committee. I was with them often early on. But then I had so much to do, somebody else had to take over the medical committee for me. As we were walking through the football season, I couldn't be the recipient of every COVID test result or problem. So I had to trust everybody to help me work through those, keep clear communication, and don't let me be surprised. When we have problems that come from someplace else, I needed a schedule of solutions. I didn't need a hundred options. I needed the three or four that could work, so we could make a decision and move on to the next one. I didn't need to know about every limitation on COVID testing. I needed to know how we could get the testing done. I didn't need a medical committee to tell me whether yes or no we could play. I needed to set an expectation that we want to try to play, and tell me how that can be possible. And that was all about saying to everybody around me: "You have to handle this part and let me know when it rises to my level."

That experience really changed the way I work, probably in a lot of good ways, and then some that I haven't been able to get back to normal, if there ever was a normal.

MACK BROWN: Crises can be the greatest thing that ever happen when you look back on it, because you forced yourself to lead in very difficult situations. Leadership is guidance when things aren't good. The National Championship teams—most of that year I just said, "Good job, that's nice." I didn't even have to coach. I had to lead. Vince Young is our quarterback. We're in his redshirt freshman year, and he only stayed three years. So this is his second year. We play Oklahoma. He's the starting quarterback. And he has a couple turnovers. We get beat 12–0 and do not score. We come back the next week and we're playing Missouri at home. You don't want to lose to Oklahoma and come back and play a home football game the next week, because they are not happy. Missouri is pretty good. At halftime, Vince had completed nine passes, four to us and five to them. It was awful. He acted like he was hurt, like he had hurt his ribs. I took him out, put him on the bench. He throws his helmet across the sidelines. I walk over and grab his arm, under the arm where nobody could see it, and I said, "I benched Chance Mock, who was the number one passing efficiency quarterback in the country to put you in, and you're acting like a baby. And you're not going back in this game. You got millions of people watching you right now. So you go back over there, and you be the best cheerleader I've ever seen, and you help us win this game, you help Chance and we'll talk tomorrow." So we won the game 28–24 and [former Texas running back] Cedric Benson ran it about every down. The next day, I bring in Vince, by myself, and I sit in a room by myself, and he is playing awful. I said, "Okay, I promised you that you would be a quarterback. I didn't promise you you'd be the starting quarterback. You're playing awful. You're trying to be Peyton Manning. You're listening to all the fans. The fans want you benched. The fans want you moved to receiver. The fans want you moved to safety. You're worried about your throwing stats, when in truth, the only stat that matters for a quarterback is your record. When you get done, nobody's gonna look up how many passes you threw. They don't care. They want to know how many games you won. So next week, I want you to practice as hard as you can. I'm going to play you against Texas Tech, and we'll see how you do. If you don't do well in that game, I'm gonna bench you. And I'm going to start Chance Mock. So you got one week to get this straightened out." So what I did was I took all of his high school highlights and said, "Look here, this is the guy I want back. I don't know where this guy's gone. I've lost him. But he was really a good quarterback." Then I took his highlights at Texas and said, "Man, every now and then he does these things. And my God, he's special. But what he's done is, he's let his family and the media and the fans get in his head, and I've lost that guy right there, and I've got one week to get that guy back." He was awful that week in practice. Just *awful*. We're getting ready to play Texas Tech, they're [ranked] tenth in the country and it's in Lubbock. They've just beaten Nebraska 70–10.

Mike Leach is the coach. It's 2004. And they've had a week off! So I'm watching him in pregame, and he's bouncing the ball halfway there. He can't complete a pass in pregame! So I figure, it's over. This is done. I've lost my quarterback. He's out of here. Well, he wins the game 52–17. He passed for 250 yards. He completed 11 of 15. And he rushed for 250 yards. And he never lost another football game in his career. So taking that crisis of losing this superstar talent, this guy who you knew had the chance to take you all the way and turn it into a positive. And no one tells that story, either. Here we are, National Championship a year later, he's 30-2, goes to the NFL, Rookie of the Year, Pro Bowler as a rookie. So many great things came out of that. And at a younger age, I probably would have just gotten mad at him, benched him, and not talked to him. Think about that.

DOC RIVERS: My biggest concern during that team meeting about Donald Sterling was, we're gonna go out and talk to the media after this meeting, and every news agency—ABC, NBC, all those big trucks, Tom Brokaw, they're all there. I wasn't concerned about Donald Sterling. I was concerned that one of my players, or someone else, would say something and *they* would become the story. I talked them into having one voice. I told them I would love to be their voice, tell me what to say. But if they didn't want me to be their voice, let's pick one voice, and they picked me, thank God. And we sat in that room and talked about what they wanted to hear. And I went out and did it. And we got through that crisis without anyone else becoming a story. Oftentimes, people want to see what the victims' reaction is, more than keeping the focus on the person who has actually done something to create a crisis. And I thought that was a very important moment in leadership, for me. Nine or ten of the players were Black. But I felt like it was even more powerful for the white players on our team. One of them made the point that [the Sterling crisis] has nothing to do with race; this has to do with racism. And we all should be upset. And it really grew our group. And it taught me a lot. You learn a lot when you're leading, if you listen. And if you pay attention.

JIMBO FISHER: I wish I would have majored in sports psychology.

JOHN CALIPARI: When you're going through it, you're also looking at: How does this change things that we're dealing with here? How does this put us more in tune to what we need to be doing? A lot of times you're dealing with a crisis with one player, within your team, and you learn that you spent so much time on that one guy that it's at the expense of everybody else. And then you learn from that experience: Why was I doing that? When I was at UMass, we had a player that I threw off the team, and my daughter Erin was about nine years old at the time, and she was going to bed and I went in and I said, "Listen, you may hear tomorrow at school that I threw this young man off the team. And she looked back at me, and she said, "Good." And I looked at her and I said,

"Good? Why did you say 'Good'?" And she said, "Now maybe you won't talk about him so much anymore." And that was my nine-year-old. So a crisis will bring about change, sometimes in yourself.

GREG SANKEY: People who have discussed leading through a crisis have said—and this is not a lament; it is an observation—there is more loneliness in that reality than I ever realized. I'd always read about it being lonely at the top. But during COVID I would have moments where I'd sit on my front porch thinking, *How in the world did I find myself in this situation?* And then it would shift to *What in the world am I supposed to do?* There were times where we had to take what was immediately in front of you, and then figure out a way to think through it. It goes back to trust and communication. On SEC campuses, I had a lot of people who in very positive ways would contribute something at a moment that they likely didn't understand the enormously positive impact it had. Arkansas's athletics director, Hunter Yurachek, sent me this quote from Colin Powell—basically, tell me what you know, tell me what you don't know, then you can tell me what you think. And we actually used that as a discussion template. Because it forced discipline. I would have these lonely moments, and then Jim Sterk, who was the Missouri athletics director at the time, would send me a podcast sermon from this church he attended in San Diego, where the speaker was talking about how David was prepared for a moment. And that showed up at a point in June 2020, when I'm waking up every day thinking, *What in the world could prepare me for this [pandemic]?* Scott Stricklin [University of Florida athletics director] sent me a message from [Pastor] Andy Stanley, who was incredibly clarified when he talked about what people need in times of uncertainty. What people need is clarity— not that you can answer every question, but give them clear statements that are actionable. And be honest about what you don't know. All of those things helped me immensely in those lonely moments when the weight mounted. I had to reconcile myself to the fact that we might not be able to play. And for our conference and our region, I knew that would be enor- mously problematic and controversial and emotional. So what I decided was, I didn't want to ever say we can't play, and then be asked questions where I said, "I don't know." I needed to do everything I could to try so that at the end of the day I could answer why we didn't clearly. And that would help me explain why we thought we could, even though I couldn't answer every question.

TOM IZZO: I had a kid [former Michigan State point guard Cassius Winston] whose brother committed suicide in November, and I had a kid whose wife gave birth to a son in the middle of February. So you talk about going through a gamut of new things to try to understand? To tell a kid, you have to miss the game—no matter what, you're *not* missing the birth of your child. Hopefully experience helps you deal with unique situations. But you have to deal with each situ- ation individually. Bring the parents in and ask how you can help. With Cassius, his dad told me I was being too soft on him. Take the kiddie gloves off. I said, "My God, I feel for the kid. He's in tears sometimes." But I've got a job to do, too, and he's got a profession to try to earn. And that helped me a lot. I will be better because of what I went through in that crisis. I do hope, though, no one else has to experience that. It was horrible. But I did learn. And I did deal with a lot on the run.

MACK BROWN: In 1999, we were getting ready to play Texas A&M, and they had the bonfire. And I'll never forget, I'm driving, and it was a Thursday, eight days before the Thanksgiving game. And I heard that twelve kids had died in the bonfire, that the fire had fallen on these kids and they had died. I pulled over. I stopped. I listened to a radio station that said if you have a child at A&M, here's the hotline to call and see if your child is okay. And then they came back and said the hotline is completely overloaded, you're going to have to drive to College Station to find out if your child is okay or not. I broke down and started sobbing, as a father of four. What an awful thing. These kids are out having fun, hanging out around this bonfire, and here we are, we've lost some of them. So here we are. What do we do? So [Texas A&M head coach] R. C. Slocum and I changed the pep rallies and tried to council kids on life and death. To this day I still have trouble celebrating Thanksgiving, because I know there are twelve sets of parents and families who lost their children. I didn't even want to play the game. We lost the game 20–16 on the last drive, and that was okay. It's one of those you remember for the rest of your life. Those are the type of things that mold you as a coach, when you have to stand up and make really good decisions in bad moments.

GREG SANKEY: I was worried about us and our student athletes at a very high level during COVID. We had a famous, or infamous, video conference with a group of football student athletes and a group of our medical folks, where there were very honest answers given. Where we knew things, we'd say what we knew. Where we didn't know things, we'd say we didn't know. There were frustrations expressed. And somebody recorded that meeting and provided it to the *Washington Post*. And that produced an article. And as a leader it was a gut punch because it was a really significant breach of trust. We were being asked questions, and we wanted to be open and honest, and we wanted to say what we knew and what we didn't know. Nobody was being required to play anything. We were just *trying*. So when I was first told of the recording, I was nauseous. And then after a few minutes I realized that that call is exactly what we *should* be doing as leaders. We *should* be answering questions as honestly as we can. When we don't know, we should say we don't know. And we should work to come back and answer the question. We shouldn't be sugarcoating anything, and where we had answers we needed to give them. I asked [SEC associate commissioner for communications] Herb Vincent to request to the *Washington Post* reporter that none of our young people be embarrassed. If you're going to print the article, which they clearly were, if there was anything that somebody said that might be embarrassing to them, that that not be used. But use the rest of it. I had no shame. We did exactly what we should have done. That's our responsibility as leaders, and if somebody is going to write an article or a perspective indicting us for leading that way, then perhaps it's their error and not mine.

ROY WILLIAMS: I think crisis management at any level, the leadership part of the guy in charge is something you have to be aware of and try to be prepared for. I've had many cases where I felt like there was nearly a crisis. And my coaches and our fans think, "Oh, that was fine, no big deal," because they didn't know everything. I put a thought for the day on the board for practice every day. I stole that from Coach [Dean] Smith, copied it straight from him. And [former UNC point guard] Marcus Paige started keeping those, writing them down every day, and putting them in a notebook and going over them each day with his mom, who had been a very successful women's basketball coach in Iowa. And Marcus said to me, anytime things got really tight or were about to go haywire, he thought that's when I was the most calm. I feel like somebody's got to be calm. I never jump up and call a time-out. I'm criticized so much about not calling time-outs. But that's the reason we practice every day—so we're prepared for those moments.

JIMBO FISHER: First half of the national championship game in 2013. We're down 21-3. That team wasn't behind all year. We were down 21-3. When there's not a definitive answer, you have to go back to fundamentals and basics. And get guys to look you in the eye. Right in the eye. And go, "Listen, what we do is right. We are good enough to do this." You have to go back to what got you here. Right now you have to stop being outcome oriented. You must be process oriented. Stay in this moment. Handle things one moment at a time. You'd be surprised how simple it is. Sometimes we overcomplicate it and eventually we become outcome oriented. We don't stay process oriented. So then you're not detail oriented enough. And then what? You're not fundamental oriented enough. The things in the game of football that are successful now were successful forty years ago, and will be successful forty years from now. That's what you must build your program on. You must build yourself fundamentally as a player, but then the psychological disposition of it, of mental toughness, play with great effort, have great discipline, have great pride in what you do and who you're doing it for. At the end of the day, that word, *grit*, to be able to sink your damn teeth into something and say, "I refuse to lose, and I refuse to do this wrong." Every time. And if you do all those things, most of the time you come out ahead. And if you don't? You can still put your head on the pillow and don't worry about it.

ROY WILLIAMS: One time I did call a time-out, and my team thought the world had ended. I told them, "Hey, I just called a time-out for you guys to understand you're the ones out here screwing it up." What the hell am I supposed to do? It was a good laugh. I wanted that reassurance for them.

PATTY GASSO: I got a phone call once late at night. One of our athletes, whose parents lived quite a few states away, was taken to the hospital. There was alcohol involved and there was a fight inside the house. The athlete was threatening to hurt herself. I got to the hospital and I just felt like *I'm now the mother of this child who is hurting.* It was an extremely helpless feeling. What do I do? I called the parents and tried to explain to them what happened. And they were in disbelief. I felt very helpless, but I was there and present, and I needed her to know that I was there. I ended up riding in the back seat of a police car with her to a mental health facility. They checked her into a room, but I was not allowed in. So I was standing in the hallway waiting for her parents, who got on a plane. It was one o'clock in the morning. I was just sitting in the hallway, feeling as helpless as I've felt in my life. But the important thing is that I was there and present for her. Presence was the key. When her parents finally were able to get there, I met with them and explained everything. It brought them comfort. Sometimes when we're helpless and can't do anything, our presence means more than words do. That was one of the most uncomfortable situations I've ever been in. But I learned it's not about me. It's not about how comfortable or uncomfortable I am. In this particular situation, it was about my presence and support, and making certain she knew I was there. My presence was me saying, *I'm here for you no matter what,* and letting her parents know that I was there. And when I say "present," I mean being all in. You care. You're not there saying, "Get me out of here, I can't stand this." It's about sitting in the hallway praying. Because that's all I could do. We're a faith-based team. We always have been. That was the only help I could give her—my prayers and my presence.

JOHN CALIPARI: One of the things that's a crisis for a coach is a bad loss. Many times, early in my career, I knew things weren't right, but we were winning. And I wasn't gonna screw that up. So I would just put my head in the sand and let it go. The problem was, when the problem did poke its head out, it would usually mean you're losing at least a couple games, and you really have to work hard to reel the team back in. I've made that mistake many times in my career. And I've done this for so long, more than thirty-five years, and that's one of those things you hope you grow out of, but you don't seem to.

ROY WILLIAMS: Our first national championship, we played Illinois in 2005. We had a fourteen-point lead at half-time, and they come back and tie the game. And we have a TV time-out, and I said, "Hey guys, did you think this was going to be easy? This is the national championship game! We're trying to win it all, here! That team down there on the other end is pretty damn good or they wouldn't be here. They have the same dreams and goals. Let's just focus. Do what we ask you to do. But it's not time to panic. Hell, winning a national championship is hard!" The guys told me that message gave them a lot of confidence. I called a time-out inside the four-minute mark. And I looked at them and said, "Guys, I don't have anything. I just wanted to let you catch your breath one last time, and let's push. Push like hell. Everything you have. Hold nothing back. The game is going to be decided in these last three and a half minutes. I trust you. I know we're going to win. Just catch your breath. I didn't bring you over here for any fancy thoughts or rah-rah mess. You're about to win a national championship." And every one of those guys said that confidence, at that time, was really important to them.

Smith's Sideline Summary: Crisis Management

- Leadership is taking crises and turning them into positives.
- The only thing that brings about real change in an organization is a crisis.
- When a crisis arises, leadership must be calm and composed, even when concerned and confused.
- Crises can become positives in retrospect, because leaders are required to lead in difficult situations.
- When crises occur, leaders must stand up and make good decisions in bad moments.
- Sometimes when we're helpless, our presence means more than our words.
- There is no textbook for crisis management.
- There's prehab and there's rehab. If you're rehabbing, you didn't handle the crisis. If you're prehabbing, you're trying to avoid the crisis. Strive to live life in prehab.

Chapter 7

SELF-EVALUATION

"Knowing others is intelligence; knowing yourself is true wisdom."

—Lao Tzu, ancient Chinese philosopher

Five words universally resonate in the quest for self-accountability and the ceaseless drive to improve: The film does not lie. A man can come up with endless excuses. He can attempt to justify any deficiency. If his denial is deep enough, he can even lie to the man in the mirror.

But when those weaknesses or deficiencies are exposed on tape for the world to see, to analyze and to deconstruct, there is no hiding.

That's where self-evaluation comes in—honest, genuine, vulnerable self-evaluation.

Where am I lacking? How do I improve my deficiencies? Why has this become a habit and to what degree is that habit limiting my potential? These are questions many of us must ask ourselves in the climb toward our peak selves.

When we're not good at something, or our performance has waned or isn't progressing as expected, or we take on a new venture that leads into uncharted professional waters, it is difficult for most of us to be honest about our inability to execute. Especially those of us who are accustomed to hard work producing success. When it's not working, it's difficult even to *watch*. I've been there.

Several years back I was asked to host a television show. The program is a two-hour monster production, shot on location on a college campus. It has a live audience, no teleprompters, and nowhere to hide.

I'd barely hosted a show before.

Certainly not a show with as many eyeballs, expectations, or moving pieces as that one. It was the cornerstone of a network. I had world-class, professional analysts to buoy me with their respected commentary and an aggressive, seasoned producer. But I was as green as a four-leaf clover with half the luck. My bosses believed deeply that I could figure out the nuance of the hosting role as we went. They weren't necessarily wrong. I did improve with time, repetition, and systematic changes to help simplify the position for me, as well as a smorgasbord of self-evaluation.

My bosses requested that I digitally record each show and take copious notes on what I did well and didn't do well. I watched each show back closely while following the show rundown, a sort of TV show script that details what is airing when, within the entire scope of the program. The rundown keeps production, direction, graphics and on-air talent all on the same page.

I despised watching those shows back. The film does not lie.

I am immeasurably embarrassed by watching myself most of the time. That doesn't mean I don't have an ego, or that I'm not proud of my work, or don't believe I do a good job.

Because I do, I am, and I believe I do.

But I hate to see my mannerisms and my quirkiness on full display. I analyze my accent, the way I form words and sentences. I loathe my cackling laughter. The whole thing.

And I know what my face looks like when I'm searching. There were times when one of my analysts offered perspective on the day's important college football games or story lines, and the director would take a stage-wide shot of all four or five of us on the panel and place it on your television screen. Sometimes I could see in my eyes that I was scrambling to find my place in the rundown, or what card I was supposed read next. That's typically something only television nerds notice, because viewers naturally focus their eyes and ears on who is talking and pay no mind to the others on the panel. It's somewhat like a football play that results in a first down: Most of us watch the ball the whole time, see the quarterback throw the pass and the wide receiver catch the pass and move the chains. We don't notice that the running back didn't pick up the blitz. But because the play worked fine anyway, the deficiency is masked and we move right along.

I'm very hard on myself. Watching those shows back each week, the good-bad ledger was weighted heavily toward negative feedback. Social media only fed that narrative. That impacted my self-confidence. I was reeling a bit. But being brutally honest with myself was educational. I had fifty people telling me how to do the job properly, many of whom cared deeply about me and my success.

I learned to not pretend.

I learned to tune out unproductive noise.

I learned to be comfortable being uncomfortable. There is no growth in the comfort zone.

That took a lot of honest self-evaluation.

I am a better broadcaster with far greater knowledge because of that honesty.

JIMBO FISHER: Self-scouting and self-evaluation is the most critical part of any program or business—and you damn sure have to be honest about it, even if you don't like what you see. *Especially* if you don't like what you see.

CHRISTIAN HORNER: In Formula 1 you have to be self-critical. It's crucial. Every two weeks from March to November in Formula 1, we're judged very publicly, globally, on our performance. So you've got to be brutally honest with yourself about that performance, and where you can improve and must improve. Races you win, you learn from. Races you lose, you learn even more from.

MACK BROWN: My self-evaluation involves other people that I trust, who I know will tell me the truth even when it's hard to hear, and ask them to give me an evaluation of what they think. I've got five or six people in my life that I really trust, who are very successful, and I ask them to constantly evaluate me and what we're doing. I send them things to look at for their opinion. I trust them, and they're very hard on me. Brutally honest. That's what I want. They've said some things to me that hurt and I took that and I dug into that personally within my own self-evaluation. It's not always pretty. But it's a must if you're going to succeed.

TOM IZZO: Are you a driven person? There are two big things I talk to my team about the last decade or so—(1) Can you self-evaluate? And (2) Can you self-motivate? If you only do one of those two it won't work. Say you're a good self-motivator but a bad self-evaluator—you're motivating yourself to something that might not be true. If you're a good self-evaluator, which there's not a lot of people who are, *and* you're a good self-motivator, then to me you can achieve an elite level.

JIMBO FISHER: Nobody is more critical of me than me. I'm very hard on myself. I constantly ask myself the question, "Is there a better way to do it?" If you can self-evaluate it means you know what you're doing. You can be attentive to the details. The people who can honestly self-evaluate and make adjustments truly understand what they're doing. There's not a lot of generalities.

TOM IZZO: The other thing I talk about with my players now to try to gain leadership, and figure out who those individuals are, are the Three *L*s: Do you *like* what you do? Do you *love* what you do? Or do you *live* what you do? And I think that to be great, you've got to be somewhere between loving it and living it.

URBAN MEYER: Self-evaluation is incredibly valuable. And to me it was very easy. Because we constantly had people critiquing our program. My friends, whether it be Greg Schiano or Chip Kelly or Lou Holtz, if someone wanted to come visit, I'd have them come in. Back when Coach Earl Bruce was alive, I'd always have him come in. And they wouldn't come in to visit, they'd come in to critique. They'd self-evaluate me and my staff. I used to call it the Yearly Audit. Just to be sure we're doing the right things, and that the culture was aligned. So I embraced self-evaluation. A lot of people don't. Because at times you don't like what you see. But it never bothered me. As much as delegation was not a strength for me, self-evaluation was.

JOHN CALIPARI: As coaches you self-evaluate after every game. What could we have done differently? What was good today? What isn't working right now? It's different for us [at Kentucky], because we got a new team every year. Players leave [early for the NBA]. So we have to fail fast. We have to be able to try things and not get stuck in the mud. If it's not working, go to something else. That's one of the things that I tell the players: You've got to be able to self-evaluate the areas you've got to get better—and be very honest about it. Guys want to shoot more until they're shooting 13 percent from three[-point range]. Why? Gotta work on it. And it's the same with turnover-to-assist ratio. You have seven times as many turnovers as assists, why would you think you're a playmaker?

Be real. Be honest. Self-evaluate honestly. Because when you self-evaluate honestly you get better.

JIMBO FISHER: If you can honestly self-evaluate, then you understand not only what you're doing, but what people are doing to you. A lot of guys can self-evaluate themselves, but that self-evaluation of yourself must entail what the other guy is trying to do to you—and your ability to have knowledge. Your ability to self-evaluate makes you continue to grow in whatever your profession is. It's always going to grow. It's always going to change and evolve. So the way people attack you is always going to grow and change and evolve, too.

NANCY LIEBERMAN: I self-evaluate in real time. I'm a spontaneous thinker. So, if I feel like I've been kind of tough on somebody, I have to recognize that in real time. And I try to always humble myself. Humility is confidence. Arrogance is not confidence. Arrogance is fake. So, I try to have humility. I have to be intuitive in my self-assessment and reflection of what energy I'm giving to the universe, and leading with love and kindness, and a smile. My smile can change somebody's day. Am I saying somebody's name in an office where nobody knows their name? That can change their day. I might put my arm around your shoulder after we hug, and that communicates warmth, caring, and friendship. In the many years I've been coaching, we wanted to be the team with the most physical touches, because those touches activate our endorphins and lets somebody know that that's a very warm, endearing thing. I have to master the things that require no talent. It doesn't take talent to be kind. It doesn't take talent to inspire somebody. It doesn't take talent to help somebody. As I think about self-evaluation, I'm probably a minimalist. As a leader, I want to help people answer their why. That's part of my self-assessment.

TOM IZZO: If you're not a phenomenal talent, like a six-eleven guy with God-given gifts, part of self-evaluation is you better live what you do. [Former Associated Press National Player of the Year at Michigan State] Denzel Valentine lived what he did. Mateen Cleaves lived what he did. I can't name a zillion people who do that. It is rare. Miles Bridges *lived* the game. He was talented, yes, but he *lived the game.* That's why he was special. He spent time and effort watching film. I ask kids, "How good are you?" They say, "I'm as good as this guy or this guy." Well, you sure as hell don't work as hard as him. There's so much trouble with self-evaluation, and it's so important. Who can self-evaluate with honesty, and who is self-driven? Now, I admit, if everybody was self-driven, I wouldn't have a job! They wouldn't need a coach!

NICK SABAN: I think the biggest thing is, you're fighting human nature. People have to understand that success is really not a continuum. It's momentary. Everybody's got to recommit to the things that they need to do to continue to improve, so that you can take on the challenge next year. And you also create something that everybody else wants to beat you. So now it's even more important for the players to have the right mindset, in terms of what you do, how you go about it, how you prepare to create the right habits, so that you can play to that high level again and have another opportunity. That's easier said than done.

MACK BROWN: I bring in other coaches and business minds to energize evaluation. Like Joe Jamail, who the field was named after at the University of Texas. He was a brilliant lawyer. So I'd sit there with Mr. Jamail and ask him anything. And I'd trust him with my life, and my God he was hard as hell on me. And it's okay. I'd take it. I'd learn from it. Red McCombs was another one. He owned the Minnesota Vikings. Coach Darrell Royal. It's usually old guys. They've seen it, done it. And I'd send them questions and thoughts I had, and everything I thought about it. And that was really good for me. Tough as hell, better be thick-skinned. But good.

JOHN CALIPARI: I've had guys who are too tough on themselves—[2011 NBA Most Valuable Player] Derrick Rose, for one. Derrick Rose couldn't stand to make a mistake. He just couldn't take it. And trying to get him to where he was better with that stuff was really important. Derrick couldn't stand turning the ball over. Couldn't stand getting beat or someone stealing a ball from him. He had to come to terms with the fact that he's not going to play perfect. You're not going to play perfect—just make sure you're playing harder than anybody you're playing against. And use the term *next.* You have to have amnesia if you're going to be a really good basketball player. Next play. Next play. Next play. If you want to be a guy who makes game winners, you can't be afraid to miss the game winner. And if you happen to miss a game winner, all you're saying is—next. I *can't wait* for the next opportunity.

TOM IZZO: You've got to have your system set up in a way that you're holding people accountable. And you're giving them responsibility. But if they don't meet those standards you've either got to be able to challenge them—back to confront and demand—or tell them there's a different job for you. I'm still working on that part of me. I'm hard enough on my guys every day that there's that expectation at this point. But I also think I need to do better. That's one thing I question that I need to do better. So here I am, ripping myself! That's self-evaluation!

MACK BROWN: Why do you self-evaluate? To keep from getting complacent. Because if you're not careful, and you're winning and doing things well, everybody's fighting to catch you, but you're not fighting to stay ahead of them. That's a hell of a challenge. Once again, you're simply trying to maintain. And maintain, to me, is an awful word. It's a disease. You've got to keep climbing. You've got to keep moving forward. You cannot maintain. Maintain, and you eventually fail.

ROY WILLIAMS: Complacency and conceit will end it. I don't think I've ever thought, *I got it made.* By God, I still go as hard as I can go. And conceit: Just when you think you're better than everybody else they're going to tell you and show you you're not. I've never had to worry about that problem because I've never thought that. But I have seen it. And I have fought it off. "We can do this, don't worry about it." Hell no! I am going to worry about *all of it.* That's a conversation I have with myself: I'll find myself saying, "Well, I don't need to do that today." And then I'll grin and nod to myself and say, "The hell I don't. Go do it."

JOHN CALIPARI: The issue with me all the time is I'll get emotional. Sometimes it's good. Sometimes it's bad. Most of the times, I have a pretty good feel where to get really emotional with the guys. But when you talk about a long season, you can't ask guys to climb the mountain every game. There's going to be games they don't play great, they're not robots. But there's times that you do insert emotion and you let them know there are certain things that are unacceptable. There are certain things that will bring out an emotion in me, and they know those things. And then you're consistent with it. And you're trying to get to their emotions sometimes. I'll sub a guy out and I'll talk about him loud enough that he can hear what I'm saying. On purpose. And he'll get so mad. I'll say, "All right, you ready to go? Get back in there." And the whole point of it is, sometimes you're in a funk and you're trying to get them going. Sometimes in a long season you get too emotional, and that's when you apologize after the game, tell them "I went overboard. I apologize. Stay with me. I'm going to stay with you." It's important that that happens, too.

LEONARD HAMILTON: I had a really difficult season recently, when my team was very young and I had no senior leadership. And all I'd learned was being tremendously challenged. My faith. My belief. My ability to communicate. It challenged every fiber, skill. How do you develop confidence, how do you believe in a system you're just now learning and haven't had any success in it? It challenges you. And you have to do it in such a way that it doesn't become offensive and turns the players off. You've got to bring them together as opposed to separating them. It's different in this era. You have to keep stats and hold them accountable for the things that matter. You can't just say, "Play hard." You have to be specific. For example: You had fifteen times to close out [defensively on a shooter]. Only 40 percent of those closeouts you had your hands up. I need 70 percent. Or, you had fifteen times to contain the dribble. You're six out of fifteen. You're supposed to front the post. You're 65 percent fronting the post. And the times you don't front the post, the ball goes in, he kicks it out and they hit the three-pointer. So you can't give them intangibles. You have to give them tangible things that they can hang their hat on and see, and at the same time inspires them to work harder and listen to your wisdom.

JIMBO FISHER: It's the responses that come back to you from players after they have left you. Or when they come back to you for advice once they've left you. "Coach, what do you think about this? We're not getting that [guidance] at the next level." And they would go somewhere and come back and say, "Coach, what we're doing now is nothing compared to what we did then." They come back and start asking me questions about how to handle certain things—"What should I do here, Coach?"—because they weren't getting that guidance where they were at. When I'm in practice with the quarterbacks, I stand behind them so I can see everything they did. And there were times when they got to pro ball and it's, "Coach, I don't get any feedback. I don't feel like I'm getting coached."

TOM IZZO: Part of self-evaluation is *show me, don't tell me.* I'm sure so many coaches have shared how valuable that is. It can be beneficial to inject your personal experiences sometimes. Vulnerability has had a tremendous impact for me. I came from a small town. I played Division II basketball. I always tell guys, "Do you want to know why I push you to the nth degree? It's because I get to do something very few people in the world get to do!" Think how many people were dreaming about what they wanted to be when [former NFL head coach Steve] Mariucci and I were sitting in our houses back in Iron Mountain, Michigan, or in college at Northern [Michigan University]. How many times do you get to dream about it, and then actually live your dream? I tell them, "Guys, me getting this job from Iron Mountain, Michigan, and North-ern Michigan University, is almost as far-fetched as you win-ning the national championship! I'm gonna wear you out to push you to live your dreams!" I want to push every player I touch—"I get to live my dream, have you really worked for it?" That's part of evaluating your own life. I was a graduate assistant until I was twenty-nine years old. People wondered what the hell was wrong with me. My mom would say, "When you gonna get married?" I'm like "Mom, I'm making $4,500 a year. What girl's gonna marry me for 4,500 friggin' dollars a year!" I laugh about that now, but that was all part of my process. I sacrificed things to get to where I dreamed of get-ting. Now, I'm not always proud of that. The reason my son is on my team right now is because I wasn't able to raise him for eighteen years. I was doing other things. I'm not always proud of those things. And I tell my guys that. I hope you can keep some kind of balance in your life. Sometimes I'm out of bal-ance. But don't think you're going to be great at everything. Because that ain't happening. You're not going to be a great dad, great husband, great coach—somebody's going to have to give something up. Listen to me: I'm self-evaluating again!

JIMBO FISHER: There's a point in self-evaluation that you have to be able to realize you're being detrimental to a guy by coaching him too hard, or being on him too much. There are times you must pull back. So, when is that? I can't tell you that. I can only tell you by the actions of the player. When they start becoming unproductive, you have to know it's time to sit them down. I like a lot of feedback from the players. "What do you like?" That allows you, when they're out of sync, to know it's time to have that difficult conversation. I call him in the office. "You're out of sync. Why are you out of sync? And what can I do to help you right now?" You flip it. It goes back to information and trust. "What do you need to get yourself back?" You feel that part out together to get back in sync. You take a step back and be honest—"This isn't working, and you're not playing to your potential. Let's figure out why, right now. Because we're in this together. My success and your success are intertwined."

ROY WILLIAMS: Coach John Thompson [former Georgetown University basketball head coach and 1999 Naismith Memorial Basketball Hall of Fame inductee] is one of my greatest mentors. He left me a message during the season once. He said, "Don't beat yourself up so much. It's counterproductive." He could tell I was pressing. When things aren't going well, I investigate the why so hard. Relentlessly. When things *are* going well, I look into the why one step away from how I look into it when it's going poorly. I'm constantly self-evaluating. That has to be continuous, every single day and every single practice. There is nobody who's harder on me than me. Oh God no. Not even close. I've been fortunate enough to win a national championship three times as a coach. And I enjoy the dickens out of it—that night. Nobody enjoys that more than me. And I'm the only person who's ever gone to North Carolina and never had a beer in five years as a student. So when I say enjoy it, I do it my own way. But the next day, the satisfaction and the feeling of getting on the plane with your guys and coming back to Chapel Hill and seeing the excitement is fulfilling. But then, that night, twenty-four hours after we win it, I'm gathering my coaches together to figure out where I need to go recruiting. I do it every year. And every year that I've won it, the first day, usually on Thursday at twelve noon, is the first time you can be out recruiting. And I make sure that at twelve noon, my butt is out there. If you want to be elite, your butt better be out there on the pulse. I don't care what your business is.

TOM IZZO: If I'm being honest, the pressure to win makes me self-evaluate. It is immense. You see a lot of people cheating because of the pressure to win, because the money is so big. I don't blame the kids for all of it. In fact, I blame myself for a lot of the way things are, because we let the kids get away with it. I always say, don't blame the twenty-year-old. Look in the mirror and blame the fifty-year-old. He's the one that's allowing this shit!

ROY WILLIAMS: There's never been a moment that validated my coaching philosophy because it's continually evolving. I'm still trying to work on it. Some things come naturally to people. When I was sixteen or seventeen years old, on Saturday mornings, I was calling everybody in the county trying to figure out where we're going to go play pickup games, and what time we should be there. And then when I'm seventy years old, I'm calling everybody to tell them what our tee time is. I'm still that guy. We have twelve couples that go on a golf trip every spring and every fall. And I'm the guy who sets up all the golf. Somebody else is in charge of the hotel, the rental cars. Granted, I'm the one who puts them all in charge, so I'm still coaching. But I set up all the golf. Where we're playing, tee times, who plays with who, what the bets are. The restaurants. I appoint somebody to pick the restaurants for dinner. But I tell them when we're leaving, who's driving, and who's riding where. It's bullshit like that I've always been comfortable with. I've always been a leader and an organizer.

For me, every single day, I do try to evaluate and decide what worked well and how the people I'm with responded. It was the same way with my players. I can't turn it off. One time I was on a recruiting call, and I told the rest of the golf group that I'd be on time, but I won't be there early. So, dinnertime comes, and everybody is wondering where we're going to dinner. One of my buddies says, "Why don't you guys just calm down. That guy's gonna walk out of that elevator in about forty-five seconds, and he's gonna tell everybody which car to get in, where that car will be in line, and where the hell we're going. So I'm just gonna sit right here and drink my Miller Lite. Us sitting here talking about it is useless." He wasn't wrong!

GREG SANKEY: Self-evaluation is among the most important elements for a leader. And not just somebody who's at the end of the hall with a C-Suite [executive-level] job. All the way up I've tried to engage in self-evaluation, and I've tried to be intentional about it. I typically use my work anniversary to look at where I am with my family, my fitness, my finances, my faith, my friendships. It's a full assessment of, where am I? What did I miss? When I came to the SEC as associate commissioner [in 2002], every year in November, on my anniversary date, I would ask myself, am I being challenged by my work role so I can learn and grow? That's part of fulfillment. That's part of culture. So for me, I go through that self-evaluation, and look at the work I do on a short term basis: was I effective in a meeting? Was I effective in leading a certain task? And then on an annual basis I go deeper, and take time to write down where I think I am. I've said to any number of students that I've worked with, when you see that I've retired or resigned from my current role, you'll realize that the challenge level had dropped, that I wasn't growing. I think where people experience burnout is not anything more than they haven't grown and been challenged in their work. And I never want that to be me.

Smith's Sideline Summary: Self-Evaluation

- Brutally honest self-evaluation is important for personal and organizational growth, even if you don't like what you see. *Especially* if you don't like what you see.
- Self-evaluation wards off complacency.
- Success is not a continuum. It is momentary. Self-evaluation is a critical piece of the commitment to improvement.
- People who can honestly self-evaluate and make adjustments truly understand what they're doing.
- Good leaders summon trusted voices to honestly critique, assess, and sometimes criticize in the self-evaluation process.
- If you're a good self-motivator but a bad self-evaluator, you're motivating yourself to something that may not be true. If you're a good self-evaluator and a good self-motivator, you can achieve an elite level.
- Don't use intangibles when evaluating. Give tangible feedback that those you lead can see and feel, and that inspires them to work harder and listen to your wisdom.
- Have thick skin. The film does not lie.

Chapter 8

EVOLUTION

"Unless you continually work, evolve, and innovate, you'll learn a quick and painful lesson from someone who has."
—Cael Sanderson, wrestler, United States Olympic Gold Medalist

"Evolve or die…If the structures of the human mind remain unchanged, we will always end up re-creating fundamentally the same world, the same evils, the same dysfunction."

This quote from the renowned spiritual teacher Eckhart Tolle speaks directly to life and leadership. Evolve or die. Like life, leadership is never static. It can, and in my opinion should, be rooted in the faith and the strength of core principles that withstand the winds of change. But it must evolve or it will not survive. As Nick Saban said in the previous chapter, success is not a continuum.

Imagine if you walked into a key presentation wearing the same haircut and sweatpants you wore to class in college. I wouldn't make it past the receptionist.

At times we are the same person from moment to moment, or even from day to day. But we are rarely the same person from year to year. Our perspective is a fluid dynamic, shaped and reshaped by circumstances, experiences, environment, relationships, triumphs, failures, joy, and hurt, and the lessons each provide. Evolution is not about core values. Evolution, ultimately, is about survival.

When I was a kid growing up back home in the Appalachian countryside, my daddy, Leo Smith, used to always say, "If it ain't broke, don't fix it." On the surface that philosophy makes perfect sense: Why change what's working? The answer goes back to what Tolle said: Evolve or die. The world evolves with every tick of the clock. Business evolves. Technology evolves. Relationships evolve. So we better evolve, too. If we don't, we're left behind. That requires an open mind to change, even if our way has always been successful and new suggestions seem uncomfortably foreign. Sometimes evolution is an important look in the mirror.

In the winter of 2018, I was at the University of Notre Dame to interview then–head football coach Brian Kelly. His Fighting Irish had qualified for the College Football Playoff, and in the days leading up to their matchup with Clemson in the Cotton Bowl, I spent time with Kelly discussing evolution.

Prior to that season, he had long been known as an angry, red-faced coach who yelled a lot, and who got worked up to a lather in a hurry.

But during that season, he was noticeably calmer. I wondered why.

Kelly explained to me that one day he was sitting at his desk in his office, mad as hell about something he couldn't recall, when he looked across the way and saw several framed photos of his family.

The photos looked beautiful to Kelly. And right then he realized he had to change. If he was going to keep coaching, he had to evolve. He told me he thought to himself, *I give my life to this game and to this job. And to do that, I have to be away from my family. My family has to sacrifice. And if I have to be away from my family in order to succeed at this job, I damn sure better start having some fun in this job and embracing the people with whom I work so damn hard.*

He stood up from his desk, walked immediately to the training room and sat down with the players getting treatment. He put his arms around them and he asked about their lives. Not just their football lives. Their lives. He sought a deeper connection. He told me it gave him clarity that was hidden before, and that clarity enabled for greater connection and trust within the coach-player relationship, and thereby within the program. Kelly has since moved to LSU—and he took the conviction to connect personally with his players with him.

KIM MULKEY: There are certain things about great leaders that will never change—and they should not change. Discipline. Accountability. Those are things that can destroy a team if you don't discipline or if you look the other way. What great leaders do is they adjust, they adapt, and they evolve. They adjust to the talents of their team. They adjust to the noise from the outside that these young people have to deal with now, from NIL [name, image, likeness] deals to social media. So leaders have to surround themselves with assistant coaches who can be in charge of those areas that a leader doesn't have time to deal with, but also understands the importance of it from a player's perspective. While we may not agree with it because of the generational gap, we always learn. We always learn what motivates young people. My players will tell you, "[Coach Mulkey] is sixty years old, she's real, she tells it like is, and she's brutally honest. But she's one of the few who has adjusted and adapted and evolved on how to motivate young people today." And that's a compliment. I take that as one of the highest compliments I've ever been paid.

DOC RIVERS: You better evolve! In all the clinics I attend, at which I talk to coaches, I use this: Beginners are open; experts become closed. If you want to be good for a long time, when you become an expert, you've got to stay open. And it's so true.

CHRISTIAN HORNER: If you stand still, particularly in Formula 1, you're going backward. You've got to keep evolving as an organization, as an individual, as a team, and as a leader. That's an absolutely crucial element, that you just can't afford to stand still, because you know that your opponents won't be standing still. And in many respects, it's the fear of failure that needs to drive you forward. Because once you've sampled success, you know what that feels like. It's like a drug. It becomes addictive. And you don't want to lose that feeling.

NICK SABAN: When I first started doing this, I was a very outcome-oriented person. And it wasn't going all that great. If you look at the record at Michigan State when I was a head coach there, it's really just a little above average. And I just said, "There's got to be a better way to do this." Then we went to Ohio State [November 7, 1998], they were number one, and I didn't think we had a chance to win. So we said, "We're just going to play one play at a time, focus on the next play, do not look at the scoreboard." And we won. So, I said, "This is a better way."

MACK BROWN: I'm a much better coach now than I was when I started thirty-five years ago. And it's for one simple reason: I'm much more direct. I'm going to say exactly what I think is the important thing that needs to be said. And I'm not going to worry about who's upset about it. I'm not going to worry about whose feelings I hurt. And the kids know that, coaches know that, our athletic director, our chancellor, our players, everybody knows it. I've found that coaches and players want that discipline. I tell a coach, "You're wrong and here's why you're wrong. And for you to get where you need to be in this business, this is something you need to do better." That's big evolution for me over the years. I wouldn't have done that at a younger age. Because I'd have been worried about somebody being mad at me, or have I hurt their feelings, or they might leave or they might run off. I'm not worried about any of that anymore. I'm worried about what's best.

DABO SWINNEY: Remaining open-minded to evolving is just the most critical thing. In business school, one of the things I learned in my graduate program is the life cycle of a business, the old bell curve: you have birth, you have growth, you have plateau, you have decline, you have death. Okay. And the reason you have stories like Blockbuster—you remember Blockbuster?—is because they plateaued, declined, and died. So the key is to never plateau. So how do we do that? People ask me all the time: "Coach, is it harder to build or to sustain it?" I always say, "I don't know—we're still building." You always start with the fundamentals. Every coach in America, when they start day one, they're gonna teach stance. Let's make sure we get in the right stance. Let's make sure we have the right foundation. It's no different as the leader of organization. We got to have the right foundation. Let's get the fundamentals right. So you assess those things, and you install those things every single year. You tear it down. I always say, "You don't get to live in last year's house. You got to start all over. And I'm telling you right now, you're gonna live in the house we build, so let's build wisely."

LANE KIFFIN: I'm sure in many businesses, but especially in football, people catch up to you. There are very few outliers who never changed and it didn't catch up to them. I say that because, with my good friend Mike Leach [former Mississippi State, Washington State, and Texas Tech head coach] just passing away, I'm reminded that what he did with the Air Raid offense doesn't happen. That is an outlier. To think that you can run the same plays for twenty years, and not looking at new ideas, same on defense and offense, that does not work except for one in a million. And somehow Mike Leach found a way to do it. We would call the plays out that he was about to run, we knew exactly what was coming, and it would still work. But everything else? I feel like you have to evolve. I've seen it eat too many people alive and they lose their jobs.

PATTY GASSO: Evolving is probably the most valuable thing you can do as a coach. And if you're not evolving, your ego is in the way. That's how I look at it. This isn't about me. This isn't about my rule and authority in the way I can make a kid feel. It has nothing to do with that. It's more about understanding where we are in this generation, and what their needs are, and how I can help. And I'm not a soft coach. I might sound nice and soft and loving, and I've had to evolve. But I still hold myself to those standards. I hold myself accountable, to hold them accountable to the standards of what it takes to be in this program. I still push. And I tell them this quite often: "I'm here to push you, because that's what you came here for. You want to get pushed. You want to win. You want to be great, and that's what I'm trying to do. I'm not the one on social media. I'm not your enemy. I'm not the one talking. I am here. I am your ally. I'm here to help you. I'm here to fight with you. I'm here for all that." But at the same time, I have to listen. I have to do my own research to know what's going on in the world and athletics, so I ask a lot of questions. I want to hear what they have to say. But I do know that the athlete word today is *time*. We don't have enough *time*. They want rest. They want peace. They want to free their minds. But part of that is something I can't control. I can't control how much they look at their phones. I just try to get them to understand the importance of having self-control, and what you're feeding into your head. And I've never had to talk about stuff like that before. That's never been an issue before. So I've had to evolve. I have to have a thumb on what is going on without trying to get in their business, and without trying to be their buddy. I think that's really important. I never had to think this way, but I'm thinking about their rest and their peace of mind and making them understand that they're valued and they're loved as the person—not the ballplayer—as the person who loves to go fishing or who loves to draw. You have to know more about them to know how to connect with them in that way, as a person and not just an athlete.

JOE GIBBS: Most good leaders would say that the willingness to evolve is very important. The football world changed roughly 30 percent every year. I came over to NASCAR, and I'd say the same thing here. You have [team ownership] charters, constant negotiations, new-generation race cars. It's constantly changing. So if you're not advancing, you're probably falling behind. And that's in any business. In a pro sport or business, you're constantly challenged by one fact: You've got to be successful. And part of being the leader, you're the person they come to for answers.

LANE KIFFIN: I do think it's very challenging to evolve when you are at the top. It's just like life—you hit rock bottom, you'll change. You have a horrible season then all of a sudden people want to change. But very few people continue to look at things when they're at the top—and I always thought that was so cool about Nick Saban; even though he's stubborn with some things, for someone at the top of the game to make the offensive [scheme] transition he made [from the traditional run-heavy I-formation scheme to an open, run-pass option scheme] says a lot. But I've known so many people that just stayed in the same offense or defense and refused to evolve, and people eventually got smart and ran them out. We were at the University of Southern California, and we were doing really well when I was the head coach there. We had Matt Barkley [at quarterback] and went 10-2. And I remember that off-season not really doing anything. We were preseason number one. Barkley was coming back. So I'm like, *Why would we change anything?* Normally we spend all off-season going to other places and looking at what's new. And I remember not doing well that next year, and I told myself, *I will never let that happen again.* I don't care how great of a year we have, no matter what, we're always going to continue to look at other methods and realize that when you do well, that means everyone's off-season is focused on you. So when you have a great season your whole conference is studying you and how to stop you. And especially when you're in the SEC, and you have such great coaches that are so smart that they'll catch you. So that's my approach to evolving. Don't assume that with all these returning players you'll be really good again.

KIRBY SMART: If you don't evolve you die. The climate changes rapidly, and you're dealing with a different landscape every year. That definitely applies to those of us in college athletics, with new rules changes constantly. But it really applies to almost all people in leadership roles. So if you don't evolve, you're in a lot of trouble. What we say around here at Georgia is this: Change is inevitable, growth is optional. Change is going to happen. Growth is your choice. And if you choose not to grow, you're going to die. Our whole evolution here has been from a control freak at the top in my leadership style, to delegating much more and we've evolved to allow more freedom in the program. That freedom comes with a lot responsibility.

KIM MULKEY: Great leaders evolve with time and get better with time. Like listening. I'm better in the area of listening than I was when I was thirty-four years old, when I became a head coach for the first time. I was immature, even though I was older and had spent fifteen years of my life as an assistant. As a leader, you may have good leadership qualities and may have done things in a positive way, but if you stay the same and you don't evolve and learn, then you become stagnant. What I may have said in a locker room twenty years ago, I may not say today. You have to evolve and understand what motivates people *right now*. Leadership is motivating people to get them to do things together at the same time, heading in the right direction. And that's so hard.

CHRISTIAN HORNER: I came into this role pretty young, thirty-one years of age. Experience gives you perspective. The biggest advantage I have now, at forty-nine years of age, versus when I was thirty-one, is the experience that comes from the knocks, the hardships, the decisions you've made along your journey—and everything you learn from them. That's a critical factor—the journey, and everything it teaches you.

MACK BROWN: Complacency will kill you. How many coaches have said that to you? I bet all of 'em! If everybody's not bought-in, you're never going to have excellence. Excellence can't exist without 100 percent buy-in. I made an awful mistake at Texas that I'll never make again by saying, "I want to maintain what we're doing." That was an awful thing to say. You never want to maintain. You've always got to be improving. You've got to evolve, not only with the game itself but with the players on your team playing the game. And I said, "Maintain." We'd win ten. We'd win twelve. We'd win thirteen. "What are you gonna do next year, Coach?" "Maintain. This is who we are. This what we're doing." And that was really stupid of me. Bad communication. That allowed us to get complacent and slip. There was no urgency to evolve and grow. Can't have that if you want to stay successful. So we reevaluate every year and every day and try to reinvent ourselves to ensure we don't have complacency anywhere.

DABO SWINNEY: I think when you start trying to sustain something, your mentality has switched, and you're gonna plateau and decline. The mindset has to always be we're always building. To do that, you always have to be in a growth mindset. What's a growth mindset? You're a lifelong learner. You're always learning. You start over every year. At Clemson, we start over every year, as if we all just met. We start over every year as if I just got this job, and I reinstall the program—the who, the what, the when, the where, the why. Every single thing we do, we take five days and we go through it. Every year. And that's an opportunity, because sometimes when you go through it, you realize there's a better way to do it now. Or you're reminded why you like that approach. And you create the buy-in because you explain the why. Not just "Here's what we do," but most importantly, "Here's *why* we do it." You have to be purpose-driven. To not plateau, you have to constantly recommit, refresh, recharge, renew, reinstall. Last year's touchdowns don't carry over.

TOM IZZO: We were discussing culture earlier. I would say our culture is ever changing. This has been a major adjustment. Every ten years there is an adjustment to be made. Social media took that to another level. Nowadays kids have to deal every moment with everybody ripping them or everybody praising them. So culturally, I do rip social media. Because I think when people can talk openly about things they don't know anything about, and it's just their opinions, those opinions become reality to these kids. They're twenty years old, man. So with my culture, I've tried to adjust and evolve a little bit, to understand better what's going on out there. I hired a social media person—because I won't get on it—to keep me abreast.

ROY WILLIAMS: First of all, I believed in everything Dean Smith did before I ever became a coach. I have a very small core. Coach Smith and [his approach] is 80 percent of what I did. There is a core group of [Naismith Memorial Basketball Hall of Fame Indiana basketball coach] Bob Knight, John Thompson and [Naismith Memorial Basketball Hall of Fame UNLV head coach] Jerry Tarkanian that I loved certain things that they did. So that's 98 percent of what I did. But I always keep that 2 percent open so I can learn something else. That 2 percent is always open for business. You can't ever stop evolving.

URBAN MEYER: I've experienced it from when I was a young coach, the way you got things done was you demanded it be done a certain way. And as the journey continued throughout the past thirty years, the way things changed and the leaders that have adapted are no longer as demanding. Earning trust is the key. If you earn trust, everything else will fall in line. Easy to say. Damn hard to do. Tough to earn. Easy to lose.

JOHN CALIPARI: An example of evolution for me is the dribble-drive [offensive system]. Listening to a junior college coach come in and tell me, "You've got to look at this." And it was so out of bounds for me, so out of the box for me, that the more I looked at it and we studied it, I said, "We're gonna go to this. And we do it with one player who could really drive." And each year we built it to have three and four guys who could all really drive, and all of a sudden my career changed. We were winning before that. We were winning 75 percent of the games. Then I went to dribble-drive, and started winning 85 to 90 percent of the games. So fate intervened there. I evolved. If not for this junior college coach who wants to come and watch a practice...afterward, we go to dinner. [(Then–Fresno City College coach] Vance Walberg was in town. Watched us practice. I said, "How do you play? What are you doing?" And those type of things have happened to me. And I've tried to take advantage of it. Be willing to look at new things, evolve, stay open-minded, even when it doesn't initially make sense.

JIMBO FISHER: Ninety percent of the people who fail, fail in the last 10 percent at the top of the mountain. That's where they die. Because they don't have the drive or the detail with everything that is required. And then, when you achieve that last 10 percent, now you're in 1 percent air. And that's what we always talk about—who's willing to keep breathing that air? Who's willing to pay the price to breathe that air? A lot of people think it. Not many live it. We used to talk about that quote all the time. Breathe the rarest air.

DOC RIVERS: When I first started coaching, when I first started playing, there were no cell phones as a player, so that meant that there was no one that could get access to your players. When you walked on the bus, everyone was talking to each other. When you walked in the locker room, everyone was talking to each other. And you walk on a bus now? Everybody's on their cell phones, listening to their individual coach, their agent, their family, their friends, and they're all telling them, "You should shoot more, you should get more minutes." That's what they hear. Now at halftime of games, before games, they're getting messages. No message that they get is a team message. I recently talked to an agent who was complaining about his client. I told the agent, "Listen, you can never talk to me again about offense. But you are more than welcome to call me about defense. If you feel like your client is not playing good enough defense, call me and let me know." It's a joke! Because you know they'll never call about defense! It's always about scoring and touches and being involved. The point there is, it's something you have to deal with. Because you're no longer just dealing with your fifteen players. You're dealing with the voices of those fifteen players, as well. So to get a guy to buy into their role, that's what I do as a coach. My job every year is to get every player to buy into their role. And the role for each player is not the same, obviously. And some people love their roles. Stars love their roles. They get to shoot every freaking time. But everyone else has to rebound. Your role is to be a rebounder. Your role is to be a defensive player. If you become a star in your role, the team can become powerful. We talk about that every day.

LEONARD HAMILTON: I believe in my heart I'm taking youngsters at one of the most vulnerable times of their life. Teenagers trying to be ushered into young adulthood, with all the distractions that come with that. And believe me, I got a whole lot of distractions that I've had to teach people how to overcome. You have to get them all together, meanwhile with someone else in their ear telling them the exact opposite of what you're saying. The way the whole climate has changed over the years, you've got to be more sensitive to how they look at things. I've had to evolve and it's not easy. I'm looking at it from my perspective. And I think I've made a couple of mistakes by not being respectful to what they think is best for them, even if it's wrong. I got kids making ill-advised decisions because they're getting their information from people with different motives than what I have. That's been a challenge.

FRANK BEAMER: We made it a point to take visits to different programs that we knew well, that were successful programs, but also programs that we had connections with. The reason we wanted those connections was because, in the coaching business, if you go to a place you don't have a connection, they're not going to truly and openly share information with you. But if you have a friend who trusts you, that's when you really get *good* information that can help you evolve your program. We got their ideas and would incorporate those ideas into our program at Virginia Tech. I agree, totally, that if you don't evolve, you're in trouble. If you're not staying right on top of things, trends, what you've learned from others that is working, then you're not getting better.

DABO SWINNEY: You fall in love with what it takes to be excellent! This is probably my number one job now: When you have so much success, people become numb to it. It's hard to win. It's really hard to win consistently. But what happens is when you're a company or a team, and you have all this success, it's easy for people to forget how hard it is to accomplish. And now, suddenly they lose their perspective and their appreciation. And when you lose your perspective and your appreciation of what it takes, you lose your joy in the journey. What it takes never changes. Greatness never goes on sale. It still takes commitment and hard work and drive and perseverance and leadership and accountability and sacrifice. And you can't get that down at the Dollar General. You gotta pay full price for that all the time. So the more success you have, the more you have to make sure you don't let the expectations be greater than the inside purpose of the program. Continue to be purpose driven, not expectation driven. And that's how you stay inside out and not outside in.

TOM IZZO: What we're missing now when guys leave early [for the NBA], is who could have been that vocal leader? Now you've got to try to *make* somebody that guy. I don't know if leaders are made. You've got to have a sixth sense to be able to read defenses. Magic Johnson could see guys behind his back. There's not a ton of those guys. So I think we, as coaches—I'm on my assistants all the time about this—I think we've got to do a good job each year of realizing, don't rest on your laurels, because this is a day and age where you have to prove it every single year. So I do think I've changed my approach. Not the principles of it. But I've changed the approach. Because each year my best players, what you'd like to be your leaders, don't come from the same cloth. So I've had to evolve in my approach.

NICK SABAN: I think back to our first national championship game at LSU in 2003. I had a tremendous amount of anxiety, because you have a team that's shown tremendous resiliency all year long to accomplish what they've accomplished, to be able to get where they are. And you really want to do the best job you can in preparation, and in how you manage the game, so that those guys have the best opportunity to be successful in the game. And I gotta be honest with you: I remember when, before that 2003 game, my son walked in the room, and I said, "I don't think I've ever been as nervous and as anxious" for a game as I was that game. It gets a little better as you evolve, and you've played in a couple of them. But then when the *expectation* becomes "you're *supposed to win*," then it kind of starts going back the other way.

DABO SWINNEY: We call it a windshield mentality. We create a mindset. Every day when we walk into our meetings, there's a huge windshield. It's about winning the day. And how do you win the day? Man you got to be in the now. Right now. Today. If you drive home with your eyes in the rearview mirror the whole way, you're gonna crash. It's important to know where we came from. We learn from that, what's behind us. But guess what? What's most important is what's in front of us. It's always about what's next. That has to be a mentality. That's how you develop competitive stamina. I've never been interested in the people who win every now and then. I've always been interested in people, and companies that win all the time. They're consistent winners. Those are the people I've tried to study. They all have the same characteristics. And one of those characteristics is, it's never about that moment, the thrill comes with "Can we go win it again?" The thrill is the journey. That, to me, is what it's all about. When it becomes just about a destination, and you achieve something, well, your eyes are in the rearview mirror. Your memories are greater than your dreams. And the people that have long-term success keep their dreams greater than their memories.

Smith's Sideline Summary: Evolution

- You either evolve or you die.
- Have a windshield mentality: Focus forward to ensure your dreams remain greater than your memories.
- Beginners are open; experts become closed. To sustain excellence, stay open.
- If you're not evolving, your ego is in the way.
- Never be satisfied with maintaining. Strive for improvement.
- These days leaders don't just manage those they lead; they manage all the outside influences of those they lead. So the leader's job is get each individual to embrace their role.
- Stay rooted in your leadership principles but keep 2 percent open for business. Never stop evolving.

FINAL SIDELINE
TAKEAWAYS

To close, it is important to share one last nugget of wisdom I received regarding the leadership approach of arguably the most successful, revered coach who ever walked this dirt: UCLA basketball legend John Wooden.

As I marched the path toward what ultimately became this project, I had fascinating conversations with some accomplished, transcendent leaders. One of those conversations took place on February 18, 2020, courtside at the Pete Maravich Assembly Center in Baton Rouge, Louisiana, minutes before tipoff of a college basketball game between the Kentucky Wildcats and the LSU Tigers. This was before I'd ever conducted a single interview or written a single word of this book. It was just an idea.

Former LSU head basketball coach Dale Brown, for whom the court on which I sat is now named, walked over to me on the purple-and-gold baseline to say hello. I told him what *Sideline CEO* looked like in my dreams, and he asked if he might reach out with some perspective.

Two days later, I received a lengthy written correspondence from Coach Brown. He shared with me that when he accepted the LSU job in 1972, he sought out experts from myriad walks of life and corners of the world to learn how those individuals achieved historic success and, more importantly, how they sustained it.

He did not stick to sports. He contacted the very best from the worlds of entertainment, public speaking, positive thinking, and, naturally, basketball.

Several names comprised each list, but when choosing the first person from whom to learn, Brown sent a request to the individual with the greatest longevity in entertainment. He contacted bandleader and TV host Lawrence Welk. Welk welcomed Brown out to California, where he detailed how he rose from tiny, isolated Strasburg, North Dakota, to the pinnacle of entertainment. From there, Brown sought out Bob Richards, a three-time United States Olympian who won back-to-back gold medals in the pole vault and then went on to become an ordained minister and renowned public speaker. Richards was the first spokesperson for the Wheaties cereal brand. Brown explained to me that he had studied Richards for many years while watching him on 16mm Wheaties films. "He was the best I had ever saw," Brown wrote.

Brown visited Richards at his Gordon, Texas, ranch, perused his library, and peppered him with questions. "We became soulmates almost instantly," Brown wrote.

For insight on how to motivate, maintain positive thinking and positive energy, Brown went to Norman Vincent Peale, author of the best-selling book *The Power of Positive Thinking*, which spent 186 weeks on the *New York Times* bestseller list, including forty-eight weeks at number one, non-fiction. Incredible. *The Power of Positive Thinking* has sold more than five million copies worldwide. "He was the father of positive thinking. He became a mentor and lifelong friend," Brown wrote.

And then there was basketball. There was no list. There was just one name. And Brown told me if he wanted to learn, he needed to head back to Los Angeles and meet John Wooden. Brown called Wooden, who immediately told Brown to come on out and visit. Brown spent four days with Wooden. In preparation for the meeting, Brown made notes. He placed each letter of the alphabet on an individual page, and asked questions about words that began with that specific letter. In his note, Coach Brown shared with me these examples:

A: What does Coach Wooden consider to be *achievement*? The first thing Wooden explained to Brown was, "Don't ever mistake activity for achievement." The two coaches discussed *attitude*— attitude of players, coaches, Wooden's attitude toward the pressure of winning, and issues that might occur with players off the court.

B: *Box-and-one defense*: Did Wooden like it? Did he respect it? What problems might it create for him when he saw it? And when he did see it, how did he attack it? *Bulletin boards*: did he have them to motivate or instruct?

C: Which *coaches* did he admire, and why? *Correspondence*: Did Coach Wooden answer all of it, or did he delegate this to someone else?

D: *Defensive drills*: Which defensive drills did Coach Wooden believe were the most effective? How long should you run them? Did Wooden practice defensive drills more often than offensive drills? What was the percentage breakdown? And was that breakdown a daily occurrence? *Diamond-and-one defense*: Did he like it? Did he use it? *Delay*: What was his favorite delay game?

E: *Education*: Did Coach Wooden hold study periods for the team, and how did he encourage the players to secure a college degree? What penalties did he implement when players were late to class, or missed it altogether?

F: *Full-court man-to-man press*: Did Coach Wooden run-and-jump, double-team, or stay man-to-man? *Fundamentals*: How many minutes per day did he spend on basketball fundamentals, and what fundamental drills did he use?

H: *Half-court zone press*: Brown wondered why Coach Wooden didn't use it as much as full-court and three-quarter-court zone press. *Halftime organization*: What were Wooden's thoughts on halftime process? Did he meet with his assistants first? For how long? Once he addressed the team, what did he focus on first?

M: *Man-to-man defense*: Did Wooden switch, fight over the tops of screens, or jump the dribbler? *Motivation*: How much motivation did Wooden incorporate?

Coach Brown knew Wooden was low-key, but what was his philosophy on motivational tactics?

O: *Offensive drills*: What were Coach Wooden's favorite offensive drills? Why were they effective? How did he use them? When did he use them? How did he integrate them within the overall scope of a practice? *Officials*: Did he believe in standing up and staring referees down? Did he believe you can intimidate refs? How did he work refs?

You get the idea. It was thorough, to say the least.

At this point in his letter to me, Coach Brown inserted an interesting expression of John Wooden's selflessness toward a young, eager coach. Brown explained that on the first of their four days together, the pair began their meeting at 8 a.m. sharp and continued through the day until about 6 p.m. After ten hours together, Brown felt he'd imposed on Wooden's time, and told Wooden how grateful he was, but that they should pause and continue the following day. Wooden cut him off. "I'm not tired," Brown recalled Wooden saying. "Sit down. Continue." Brown wrote: "Coach Wooden never seemed to tire. I stayed that first day until 10 p.m. He was a human dynamo."

The alphabet sessions continued to include passing drills, recruiting, scouting, scheduling, time-outs, conference and NCAA tournament preparation, weight training, and why Wooden frowned upon zone defenses.

It was a four-day basketball master class.

One day, Brown said, he and Wooden were walking toward Wooden's office and some UCLA players were running a full-court pickup game inside UCLA's legendary arena, Pauley Pavilion. As the two walked the sidelines of the court, one of the players—Brown recalled it being Larry Farmer— drove toward the hoop for a layup, and laid the ball up over the rim. Wooden stopped in his tracks, looked at Farmer and calmly stated, "Larry, lay the ball up on the backboard as you were taught."

"That was all he said, and that was all that needed to be said," Brown wrote. "And all Farmer said was, 'Yes, sir.' That was another example of Coach Wooden's attention to detail."

The last day Brown was in Westwood, he went to Wooden's home to thank him for being so gracious with his time and tutelage. When he was leaving, Brown said Wooden offered some parting words: "Well, Dale. I'm really glad that you came out, and it's been a delightful time. However, it wouldn't have been necessary for you to waste your time and money, and all those pages of notes you took. Because if you do the following three things, you will be successful in major college basketball, and if you don't do the following three things, it will be most difficult." Brown noted that, in typical Wooden fashion, the great coach didn't say "impossible," rather "most difficult."

Brown scrambled for his pen.

These three things are fairly simple, Wooden began.

Number one: Make certain you always have better players than anybody you play.

Now, with that established, number two: Make sure you always get the better players to put the team above themselves.

And number three, this is very important: Don't try to become some coaching genius or give your players too much information. Always practice simplicity with constant repetition.

That initial meeting would not be the last time Coach Brown visited Coach Wooden. The pair maintained a friendship for the next thirty-eight years. Brown loved going out to California to sit and listen to Wooden tell stories, recite poetry, and relay razor-sharp wisdom until Wooden passed away in June 2010. Wooden was ninety-nine years old.

Brown understood immediately that John Wooden would be among his life's most significant leaders and mentors.

"He was a teacher. He was a mentor. I can remember many, many times sitting in his house and the phone would ring, and it would be someone who had always wanted to meet him. He would invite them over. One day, the phone rang and it was the national basketball coach of Spain. Coach Wooden said, 'Come on over.'" [Wooden's number was listed in the phone book, Brown said.] "You didn't have to be a celebrity to enter his house. He wasn't the kind of person who tried to display his knowledge. People from all walks of life and from around the world sought him out for his knowledge, simplicity, and sincerity. Every time I left his presence there was something new I had learned."

Outside of Bill Walton, Brown believes he's heard more Wooden quotations and phrases than anyone. Brown will tell you he used Wooden's teachings throughout his forty-four years of coaching, "only not nearly as well." Brown says the greatest lesson he learned from John Wooden is this:

> "Love what you are doing every day, and love people. I can remember many times when someone was refilling his water glass for him in a restaurant, and while everyone else at the table just keeps talking, Coach Wooden would always stop and say thank you. He was loaded with love. He seldom brought up religion or spirituality. Because he lived it. He was always teaching by example."

Brown closed his letter to me with this, his personal tribute to John Wooden:

> "My dear friend John Wooden is truly an American treasure. He was kind, caring, highly intelligent, vibrant, strong-willed, principled, humble, and one of the most fascinating men of this, or any, generation. Why was the greatest coach who ever lived like this, and not egotistical, selfish, arrogant and greedy, like so many that reach the pinnacle of what the world often defines as success? It is because he firmly believed in what the first *Webster's Dictionary* ever printed, in

1806, described as success: fortunate, happy, kind and prosperous; not how dictionaries define success today: attainment of wealth, fame, and rank."

Coach Wooden's definition of success says, "Fame, fortune and power are not success. Success is peace of mind, which is the direct result of self-satisfaction in knowing you did your best to become the best that you are capable of becoming."

Brown detailed that he'd also heard Coach Wooden say on several occasions that the four things mankind craves most are freedom, happiness, peace, and love. And that none of those can be obtained without first giving them to someone else.

The best way Brown knows to describe Wooden is that every time he left Wooden's presence he felt better about mankind and carried with him a quest to become a better man.

"Perhaps, a better way to define Coach Wooden is what Einstein said about Gandhi: 'Generations to come will scarce believe that such one as this, ever in flesh and blood, walked upon the earth.' Now that Coach Wooden has left this earth, I ask myself how can I ever thank him for being my friend for 40 years? And as usual, my answer comes from the words of Coach Wooden, himself. In the last letter I received from him he said, 'Although "thanks" is a rather simple, one-syllable word that too-often is used without true feeling, when used with sincerity no collection of words can be more meaningful or expressive.'"

What a profound perspective on gratitude. "Thank you" is validation. Often, it is all anyone hopes for in return for their kindness, effort, passion, care, or time.

With that, I want to thank you so much for reading *Sideline CEO*.

> I look at a coach like a racehorse jockey. I've never been on a racehorse in my life, but if you threw me up on Secretariat, I could probably win a race. That's what you win with; you aren't going to outcoach anybody. If they have better players than you, they're going to beat you. If you have better players than them, you're going to beat them. Coaching comes into play when things are fairly even.
>
> —Steve Ragsdale, Virginia High School League
> Hall of Famer; three-time state champion
> head football coach, Giles High School (Va.);
> the author's high school football coach

Thanks for running with a bunch of farm boys, Coach. Steve Ragsdale was my high school football coach. Most of the young men he led were not thoroughbreds. I certainly wasn't. There were times when the other team had more horses. But nobody ever outworked us. That's a lasting lesson. That foundation goes all the way back to the initial lesson in this book: Push them beyond what they believe is possible. As the months progressed during this project, and the interviews and insight accumulated, I was reminded how deeply my coaches impacted me. I carry them with me. Not just their tutelage but their spirit. I am so grateful for them. As leaders they pushed and pulled and cussed and cared and believed in my teammates and me.

They had license to push and pull and cuss and care *because* they believed.

We are human. We succeed and we fail. We make mistakes. Environmental inputs produce emotional outputs. We feel belief. And we feel doubt. Because time is so precious, time invested in the human spirit is emotional currency. My coaches invested countless time. Most coaches do, no matter the age group, level, or sport. Everybody who ever played for Coach Ragsdale could spend an hour detailing his influence on their lives. He was an educator of high esteem. Complex mathematics. Calculus. He considered himself a teacher first, a coach second. I appreciate that very much. But if I'm being honest, he taught me far more on that old dirt-patch-hilltop cow pasture we called a practice field than he did on any blackboard in any classroom.

I don't remember a single calculus principle from the classroom. But I remember every metaphorical life lesson from the locker room.

I think about my coaches often. They shaped us. Hell, they helped raise us. They demanded effort and respect from my teammates and me. They cussed us when we needed it. And our parents expected them to. They held us accountable. They injected life perspective into every drill and every practice. They taught us that vital lesson Nick Saban and John Calipari discussed: Elite preparation results in playing freely, process over outcome, play to your training. Playing free allows for no anxiety, and results in the *joy of winning* rather than of the *relief of winning*. Thirty years later, I'm still learning to apply that approach to my daily walk. I spend far too much time considering the impact of the outcome, when I know in my soul it's already written, anyway. Scottie Scheffler, the 2022 Masters Champion, stopped me in my tracks the evening before he won the Green Jacket. Standing outside the press building at Augusta National Golf Club, I asked him how deeply he had allowed himself to consider the historic impact of winning the Masters. He told me:

> "If I win this golf tournament, it will change my life on the golf course. But it won't change my personal life at home. Winning the golf tournament isn't going to satisfy my soul or my heart. I know that going in, so I am able to play freely, knowing that the rest isn't really up to me. I'm just going to do my best."

The principles in this book are applicable in our daily walk. I try every day to be a great leader in my home. As a parent, I am transparent with my children. When they make a mistake, it is almost certain I've made the same mistake at some point during my journey. I confront their mistake. I demand corrections and lessons learned as they progress forward. But I don't just tell them, I show them, by detailing the moments during which I made the same mistake. I don't tolerate laziness. Pick up after yourself. Do your job as part of our team. To sustain harmony in our home, it takes all five of us doing what's right, not what's easy. To me, this speaks directly to Saban's thought about high achievers and mediocre people. I have license to demand self-accountability, because I've invested time, energy, and care into every aspect of my children's lives. And with that, they know what I tell them is in their best interest, even if they don't like it. And with Lainie, I get her opinion on virtually every decision; we discuss scenarios and create game plans. I would call her my offensive coordinator, but that would be inaccurate. The fact is she's the head coach under our roof. Her strategy and preparation enable us to win.

The principles in this book apply to corporate America, too. I believe excellence lives at the intersection where preparedness meets passion. I try through kindness, effort, preparation, and passion to find and grow my best self, so that I do not limit my colleagues, producers, camera operators, and interview subjects in the effort to be their very best.

Ultimately, these lessons are something like the lyrics to "My Song Will Never Die," cowritten by country music icon Eric Church and delivered beautifully by another country music icon, Luke Combs:

When I hear that hallelujah chorus calling me back home
I'll lay down this guitar and someone else can sing my songs
It ain't about the leaving, it's in what you leave behind
I will, but my song will never die.

These lessons will live on long after those who issued them do, long after I do. Because after we're long gone, trust, clear communication, keen listening, empowerment through delegation, great culture, brutally honest self-evaluation, and the willingness to constantly evolve will define great leaders.

ACKNOWLEDGMENTS

The list of people within this project and surrounding this project to whom I am forever indebted is long and distinguished, most notably the book's foundation—the coaches who offered me time, insight, perspective, and vulnerability.

To Frank Beamer, Mack Brown, John Calipari, Tim Corbin, Jimbo Fisher, Patty Gasso, Joe Gibbs, Leonard Hamilton, Christian Horner, Tom Izzo, Lane Kiffin, Nancy Lieberman, Urban Meyer, Kim Mulkey, Doc Rivers, Nick Saban, Greg Sankey, Kirby Smart, Dabo Swinney, and Roy Williams: Thank you for sharing so openly, and trusting that I would carry your words and actions to the masses in an inspiring and accurate way. You are titans of your profession. Your wisdom is priceless. Your time is precious. Thank you so much for giving me so much of both.

Writing a book like this, one that is truly comprised of others' words far more than your own, it is imperative to confirm details, context, fairness, and accuracy. I wore these coaches out. In the name of due diligence, I went back to many of them multiple times to ensure I got their words right. I'm certain my badgering annoyed them at times. None of them blinked. I am grateful for that.

To the sports information directors and team communications officials who helped me arrange that precious time with those legendary leaders, thank you for patiently navigating my requests.

To Tim Tebow, for taking the time to write such a thoughtful, meaningful foreword for *Sideline CEO*. Tim's influence in my life is vast. He is a natural leader. His conviction to serve others has changed my perspective and led me toward a servant leadership approach in my own daily walk. Tim is better at it than I am. He is the busiest person I know. He really did not have the time to sit down and write considerate, kind words about this project. But he made the time. That's Tim. Thank you so much, brother.

To Lainie, thank you for patiently listening to my consistent insecurities about a project's potential resonance or merit, and for always reminding me that the beauty is in the journey and the fellowship with the individuals involved. The blessing is the opportunity to impact lives with lessons, and even one life impacted is a victory. (Plus you remind me that I get to write another book!)

In its own way, your tutelage is process over outcome. Saban would be proud. Above all, thank you for loving me and accepting (and tolerating) all that comes with that.

To Cambron, Mia, and Vivian, thank you, once again, for sharing your daddy with so many other people, all the time. You three teach me key life lessons every day, and you inspire me to continually seek the best version of myself. I'm so grateful I get to be your dad. Always remember: If you live life with a compass that points toward kindness, effort, and passion, you will never go wrong. The opponent is not always the obstacle. The opponent is the person you were yesterday. Spend each day working to defeat that person, and you will continue to thrive. I love all of you so much.

To my sister, Stacy, thank you for always being enthusiastic about my adventures and supporting my work. I love you and I'm proud of you. Mom and Dad are too. They'd be tickled to death by what we've made of ourselves. We done good, kid. If I were a betting man, I'd wager you'll use some of this insight with Nicholas, as well as your teachers and students—especially Coach Beamer's.

To my extended family on the Cocozza side, Don and Sally, Donnie and Farrah, Mike and Brooke, Lia and Shaun, Bethy and Matt, Andi and Marco. and all the nieces and nephews, thank you for loving me like a brother. I made sure to put a Philly coach in this book just for y'all. (And Doc was damn good, too.)

To Creative Artists Agency, specifically my daily support team, Matt Kramer, David Koonin, Marco Critelli, Sydney Lipsitz, Katherine McConnell, and David Larabell, thank you. Your constant, tireless work on my behalf, your foresight, and your willingness to fight like hell for me is vital. I am grateful for you.

Sean Desmond and everyone at Twelve, thank you for continuing our fruitful partnership, and offering me once again the platform to grow my dream as an author. Your belief in me matters. I am grateful for you.

To the believers, and my amazing network of friends: Your support is critical. You're the middle finger in my fist. You hunker down and fight when I need it, and you extend yourself on my behalf when asked. I am grateful for you.

And last, to my own coaches, Steve Ragsdale, John Howlett, Bruce Frazier, Dave Witt, Randy Roe, Alan McGraw, James Rogers, Stevie and Danny Dickerson, and Gary Rundles, I carry you with me. I was unaware of it when you had me, but with age I began to realize the time you invested in me was precious. It was time you could have been doing something else—anything else—far less taxing than trying to corral a bunch of teenage boys, teach them the power of shared sacrifice, effort, teamwork, and selflessness, and how to win gracefully and repurpose the disgust of failure into fuel for the future. You taught us to play for something bigger than ourselves.

I am grateful for each of you. Thank you.

ABOUT THE AUTHOR

Marty Smith has produced in-depth interviews, vulnerable storytelling, and breaking news reporting across every ESPN platform for nearly twenty years and in almost every sport, including college football and basketball, the NFL, NBA, NASCAR and IndyCar, Formula 1, the horse-racing Triple Crown, the Masters, and the PGA Tour. Marty's 2019 memoir, *Never Settle: Sports, Family, and the American Soul,* is a *New York Times* bestseller.